EVERYONE
IS A SUPERMODEL

Secrets For Any Career Based On My Modelling Experiences

KELI LENFIELD

published by

LUCKY
PINEAPPLE
BOOKS

ISBN
978-0692405352

TABLE OF CONTENTS

WHY DO WE HAVE POOR BODY IMAGE? WHY DID I?

The phrase "body image" was first coined by an Austrian neurologist and psychoanalyst, Dr. Paul Schilder, in his book, *The Image and Appearance of the Human Body* (1935). In it, he explains that "Human society has at all times placed great value on beauty of the human body, but a person's perception of their own body may not correspond to society's standards."

So, society is the reason we have body image issues? Again with the ridiculous notion of comparison?

Part of my modelling career was in Paris when I was living there as a student at the Sorbonne University. Just as my career started to take off, a new face emerged on the scene, which changed everything. Her name was Kate Moss and the waif/heroin chic look was born. My agent put me on orange juice and water for three months. Bulimic and still deemed "not thin enough" by the industry, the hip bones had to go, figuratively speaking, and I was born with an arse – how dare I! So, that was that. 19 years old, on my way home smoking cigarettes, much to my family's horror, as one very sick little girl. Male models are not safe either when it comes to body image expectations.

The modelling industry is all about comparison – if you have "the look," you are employed and able to pay the rent, smoke and drink and eat (occasionally). In the real world, comparing yourself is just unhealthy – full stop! You will never be another person because you are you. Your DNA is unique. Your experiences and your perception of those experiences is unique, as is your perception of your environment, your upbringing, your values, morals, standards, achievements, weaknesses and attitude towards all of this. In my humble opinion, we have become a *society* that is constantly on trial – trial by media, trial by peers, trial by our own comparative expectations. There is unnecessary and unfair pressure applied when one is trying to be someone or something else. The judgement and diversity rests solely on your shoulders, if you wish to carry it.

Why is it that an article about a stunning woman who has managed to achieve, feel, live and survive loss has to also mention that she's (gasp!) … a size 14 or 16? Like her size or "fuller figure" is a major contributor to achieving, contributing and surviving?! What about just simply applauding her achievements, inspiration and contributions to others?

Does this bother anyone else or just me?

Take the cultural angle and treat yourself to a viewing of Renoir or Toulous-Lautrec's magnificent paintings, go and see a movie starring our very own Rebel Wilson or read Dawn French's autobiography, *Dear Fatty*, or better still, Naomi Wolf's *The Beauty Myth*, and appreciate where we came from and what we all are able to achieve, endure, create and suffer, no matter what size or shape we are.

Change your thinking, people! Why should what you look like mean so much? What makes you think that by looking like someone else, you will *feel* better? Our bodies eat, sleep, create, inspire, heal, nurture, protect, move, function, breed and breathe. That's what they are there for. So with so much good food available to us, why would you want to eat crap, or worse still, starve yourself, in order to try and look like someone else?

Please note that I am not minimising the severity of eating disorders and the plight experienced by way too many boys, girls, men and women. There is help readily and privately available, and you do not have to live your life as others dictate you should.

Eating disorders are a mental illness and there is a cure. In 2013, I went to Brisbane and attended a workshop provided by The Butterfly Foundation on Eating Disorders presented by Paula Kotowicz. Paula is a counsellor who used to work closely with the foundation and specialises in eating disorders and body image issues. I found her workshop enlightening and frightening. The attendees consisted of teachers, mothers, friends, trainers, course developers and past and present sufferers, all in one room. The energy was overwhelming, to say the least. I recently coordinated a Google hangout, where I asked Paula her professional opinion on these subjects, as well as a number of other topics, such as the "D" word, common misconceptions and her definition of perfectly imperfect.

The full hangout, titled "Perfectly Imperfect," goes for just over 50 minutes on YouTube. It was our first live hangout and a very frank and professional discussion from both of our points of view and experience. I was surprised by some of her findings.

Yes, models and dancers definitely suffer from eating disorders and body image issues, but the majority of cases are from things happening in the home, such as failed relationships, family dynamics and environmental factors, or anything as a repercussion of despair, guilt, depression, shame or disgust.

Adolescents are mainly concerned with body image and being accepted. Not being thin enough in most cases equates to not being attractive enough and they are comparing themselves to common imagery. Paula aims to rebuild the sufferer's sense of self acceptance, self awareness, self compassion and self forgiveness, whereby the disease cannot exist in these conditions. Thin is quite often seen as clever, attractive, pretty and successful, while obese is seen as the complete opposite of all of these traits.

The most dangerous difference between bulimia and anorexia is that anorexia is recognised in a very short amount of time, mainly because its symptoms and effects are obvious to the eye. Bulimia on the other hand takes up to 10 years to present treatment – one very hard habit to break and not always obvious.

We are really busy NOT being ourselves! The driving force is the thin ideal that we receive in copious amounts of volume from a number of sources. We are surrounded by it and cannot avoid it. We have constant access to the misrepresentation of people who appear to be perfect. The shift is that we are expected to look like the people we are seeing. These images are presented in a way that everything is Photoshopped out (no pores, moles, scars or smile lines allowed!), the diets are horrendous and external beauty is revered…and to make matters even harder, youth is beauty.

The natural state of eating has been community sanctioned to the point where cravings, which are your body's way of letting you know what it needs, have been put into a good/bad category and eating has become a controlled and disciplined habit. You are judged by how you resist temptation and how you respond to food and consequently produce inappropriate feelings of guilt if you do actually listen to what your unique, one-of-a-kind body wants and needs.

At one time or another, we have all succumbed to some type of dysfunctional eating habit.

Please, as a fully recovered bulimia sufferer, if you or anyone you know is suffering from an eating disorder, help and support are available. An eating disorder is a psychiatric illness with very serious physical complications. They can be treated and recovery is possible, but it is vital that you get help! If you or a friend need a list of resources, please see my notes at the end of the book.

THE FABULOUS YOU!

Skill #1: Shape Up Your Body Image

"No matter what size or shape you are, you can always wear a white shirt, jeans and a Chanel jacket." – Karl Lagerfeld, fashion designer

CELEBRATE! You ARE perfectly imperfect! Love it or…

No, just love it! You have a beautiful body.

Don't believe me? Fine. Believe yourself! Yep, I'm turning all the responsibility of body love and ownership over to you, the body owner! Celebrate your unique shape and embrace it. Amen.

All body shapes are timeless. The hourglass shape always reminds me of Ms. Marilyn Monroe. The rectangle shape is 1920's and 30's glamour (think *The Great Gatsby*). There is so much fabulous fashion and choices available today, you can look and feel fantastic quite easily by **learning**

about and **accepting your** body shape - its easy, it's fun and so worth it!

Here are some supermodel secrets you can apply to your own body:

* Love it! Forget about anyone else – models do! Love it and <u>learn</u> what looks good on you. I'm talking about clothes and accessories!

* What is your body shape? Each one is as gorgeous as the other and by the way, just in case you forgot, you were born this way! Not good enough? Give yourself an honest answer as to why, WITHOUT comparing yourself to anyone else.

* Check out websites dedicated to your body shape, such as shopyourshape.com. This is one of the best sites to find what body shape you have and what styles, colours, cuts and trends will compliment your shape. Their tagline is: "It's your shape, not your weight, that matters!" Gotta love

that!

But what *is* your shape?

While I've got your attention, let's spend some time on dressing for your shape. What shape are you, men and women?

Men can be a **triangle, inverted triangle, rectangle, oval** or **trapezoid**. The **triangle** has a narrower upper body than lower body. The **inverted triangle** is the reverse: broader shoulders with a smaller hip area. The **rectangle** shape's shoulders match the hips. The **oval** figure has narrow shoulders, gains most of the weight in the midsection and has thinner upper legs. The **trapezoid** has broader shoulders, narrowing down in the waist like most fitness models.

Women can be an **inverted triangle**, a **pencil** (or lean column), a **rectangle**, an **apple** (sometimes called round), a **triangle**, a **neat**

hourglass or a **full hourglass**. An **inverted triangle** has wider shoulders and narrower hips. A **pencil** is a thin and long rectangular shape. A **rectangle** is a shorter, slightly wider version of the the pencil. The **apple** means you gain all of your weight in your midsection and have thin, long limbs. A **neat hourglass** can be very thin or very curvy, but the commonality is all sizes have a tight shape. A regular hourglass, or **full hourglass** shape, is a curvier type of hourglass, like Christina Hendricks.

Classic Wardrobe Pieces

These are items of clothing that you should always have in your wardrobe and never throw out (unless of course, they have been worn to death and need replacing!). They are timeless pieces that will always be in fashion and go with anything.

The list:

For women:

* Anything well tailored that fits you like a glove and you are not constantly adjusting when you are wearing it.

* Good quality jacket or blazer.

* Classic Little Black Dress (LBD), which well and truly covers your bum!

* Well cut and well fitted denim jeans (no holes).

* 3 T-shirts and singlets/camisoles (black, white and grey).

* Crisp white tailored shirt (preferably with a collar and cuffs).

* Pearl and/or diamond stud earrings.

* Hoop earrings (ones that don't divorce the size of your entire head!).

* Good quality flat shoes (not scuffed or marked and polished).

* Classic black high heels (not scuffed or marked and polished).

* Silver or gold watch.

* Patterned stockings.

* Quality cotton summer dress.

* Good quality summer sandals (black, white, bronze, silver, neutral or gold).

* Favourite clutch (preferably leather).

* Tailored pencil skirt to just above the knee.

* Tailored shorts (mid thigh).

* White canvas shoes. The best thing about these is they are machine washable and can stay white for longer.

* Classic overcoat, such as a trench or peacoat.

* Cashmere blend cape or wrap.

For men:

* Good quality jacket or blazer.

* 3 T--shirts and singlets (black, white and
grey).

* Well cut and fitted denim jeans (no holes).

* High quality suit, either single or double
breasted – whatever suits your shape.

* Neutral chinos,

* Good quality leather shoes (black and
brown).

* Good quality brogues, loafers and/or
slides.

* Good quality watch.

How to dress for different events

First and foremost, you need to think about
why you are going to a particular event. Who will
be there? What kind of an impression do you want
to make? And what outcome do you want to
achieve?

Secondly, always dress so you are comfortable but appropriate. It is important that you display your personality in your dress choices. More often than not, distinctive accessories will get you noticed and even be an ice breaker for a conversation. But always remain polished, pay attention to detail and smile.

Some dress code definitions:

A **Black Tie** invitation calls for formal attire. Men wear tuxedos, women wear cocktail dresses, long dresses or dressy evening separates. A little black dress is completely appropriate for black tie functions.

Formal usually means the same as black tie, but in some trendier cities like New York or Los Angeles, it could mean a black shirt and no tie with a tux. Women wear cocktail attire, long dresses or dressy evening separates.

A **White Tie** or **Ultra Formal** invitation requires that men wear full dress, with a white tie, vest and shirt. Women wear long gowns.

A **Black Tie Optional** or **Black Tie Invited** gives you the option of wearing a tuxedo or formal dress, but it should clue you into the formality of the event, meaning a dark suit and tie would be your other option. Women wear cocktail attire, long dresses or dressy evening separates.

Creative Black Tie leaves room for trendy interpretations of formal wear. He can go more modern with a tux -- maybe a black shirt, no tie. She wears long or short dresses or evening separates.

Sometimes, themed parties call for dress codes like **Creative Black Tie**. In that situation, you can have more fun with it, choosing a dressy look with a theme. For example, for him, it could be a tux with boots. For her, it could be a long dress paired with a Southwestern style silver belt and jewellery.

Resort Formal is a designation for warm weather locales (like a beach wedding), where the women can wear something bright and lightweight, a floral sundress for example.

Semi-Formal, or **After Five**, means that tuxes are not required, nor are long dresses. An evening wedding, that is, anything after 6 pm, would still dictate dark suits for him and a cocktail dress for her. Daytime semi-formal events mean a suit for him and an appropriate short dress or dressy suit for her.

Business Formal is the same as **Semi-Formal** for him, but for women, it suggests that women opt for more tailored dressy suits and dresses. The idea is to still be business appropriate –

which means nothing too sexy or slinky – but still dressed up.

Cocktail Attire means short, elegant dresses for her and dark suits for him. The little black dress is the ultimate cocktail dress and appropriate for most special occasions.

Informal is often interpreted as the same as **Casual**, but it actually calls for the same dress as **Semi-Formal** – dark suits for him, short dresses for her – especially when associated with a wedding or special event.

Festive Attire is usually seen around the holidays, with the mood of the party being.

Informal or **Semi-Formal**. For her, it means to choose looks with a bit of sparkle or holiday bent (i.e. a beaded sweater with black pants, a red silk blouse with a black skirt).

Dressy Casual calls for dressed up versions

of casual looks. For him, it could be trousers and a sports coat. For her, a dressy pants look. Jeans, shorts, T-shirts and other casual looks are not appropriate.

Casual generally means anything goes, including jeans, sneakers, etc. If the host or hostess wants a more dressed up approach, it would be dictated on the invite.

Wedding Guest Styles for Her

Informal Daytime: Short dress or suit. Business attire is OK for morning weddings.

Informal Evening: Cocktail dress, which is any dressier dress – for example, a little black dress – that's not full length.

Semi-Formal Daytime: Short dress or suit.

Semi-formal Evening: Cocktail dress.

Formal Daytime: Short dress or suit. Hats and gloves optional, although it's rare to see hats and gloves at most weddings.

Formal Evening or Black Tie: Long or dressy short cocktail dress (beading, glam accessories, wrap, etc.).

Ultra-formal or White Tie: Long gown, extra glitz (furs, diamonds, etc.).

Wedding Style for Him

Informal Daytime: Dress shirt and pants, preferably a sports jacket.

Informal Evening: Suit.

Semi-Formal Daytime: Suit.

Semi-Formal Evening: Dark suit.

Formal Daytime: Dark suit and tie.

Formal Evening: Tuxedo (if invitation states Black Tie), or dark suits if women wear short dresses.

Ultra-formal Evening or White Tie: White tie, vest and shirt.

Grooming

Dos and Don'ts for Her

* Don't wear white because it competes with the bride. There are plenty of other colours available. This rule may seem outdated, but it's actually just good etiquette to not compete with the bride on her special day.

* Don't worry about wearing the same colours as the bridesmaids or mothers. You can't possibly coordinate with everyone in the wedding party.

* Do wear something feminine and appropriate, out of respect for your hosts. Club wear, overtly sexy clothing (strapless, see-through, etc.) doesn't belong at a wedding. If you have to ask if it's appropriate, it probably isn't.

* Don't wear opera length gloves (to top of the arm) with anything but sleeveless or strapless gowns.

* Do take off your gloves to eat or drink.

* Do use good judgment if the invitation doesn't specify the formality of the event. A pastel suit or soft floral dress for daytime or a little black dress for evening (after 6 pm) will take you almost anywhere.

* Use good judgment when it comes to getting dressed. Casual can mean a pretty sundress for a coastal or beach wedding, but it rarely means something as sloppy as jeans or shorts.

Dos and Don'ts for Him

* Don't try to get cute with a tuxedo. A black tux with a white shirt and black bow tie is the best way to go. If Creative Black Tie or some sort of other vague formal description is used, then going with a tux and black shirt and no tie, might be acceptable.

* Do wear a dark suit, with a tie if the wedding is after 6 pm and doesn't say Black Tie.

* Don't wear a tuxedo during the daytime, regardless of the formality of the event.

* Do use good judgment if the invitation doesn't specify the formality of the event. A dark suit and conservative tie will take you just about anywhere.

* When in doubt about what to wear, remember you can always ask the host or hostess what they expect party guests to wear.

* In my opinion, if you have used good judgement, you can never be overdressed!

Remember:

Eat well as best as you can, so when you do indulge (which you should every now and then), you and your body will enjoy it. Supermodels try to feel good. If that means they go for a run, meditate, swim, box or climb (you get the idea), they <u>feel</u> <u>good</u> about themselves, which in turn keeps their bodies looking and feeling healthy.

Balancing your weight-feel good-health ratio is a result of what you eat *plus* what you do. Yes, exercise of some description is required, honey! Find something you enjoy doing, no matter how basic, and make it part of your weekly routine.

About diets…

FYI: The D word, diet, is forbidden in this book and any future publications! Except in this one and only circumstance where I would like the opportunity to explain why it is forbidden.

Plain and simple, I don't believe in them AND I strongly believe that as much as any type of motivation to improve your health is a good thing, the only ones who gain anything from the diets, in their most commonly known forms, are the companies that create the "miracle" products and the celebrities who endorse them. Trust me, if we all had our own personal chef, masseuse, trainer, stylist, nutritionist, physician and makeup artist (not to mention a couple of million in the bank!), would you really, honestly give a toss what other people thought, and more importantly, how would you feel about yourself?

Everyone is made up of their own unique DNA code. With this code comes different metabolic rates, genetic strengths and weaknesses with regard to organs, tissue formation, cell renewal, bone density, digestion, growth patterns, hormone levels, weight balance and overall development, stress coping capabilities and personalities. What works for some certainly doesn't work for others.

For example, my biological mum and I

could not be more different. Do you know what she does? Mum finds food boring, has tried every diet available and paid a lot for it (sometimes twice), doesn't believe she has cravings and eats everything on the plate even when full. She is attracted to the sugar, cream and carbs when tired, excuses herself about exercise, eats too much when stressed, ignores digestion issues and has seen her weight fluctuate and increase since having kids. She is an hourglass body shape at 5'8".

My only "diet" was when I was modelling. Need I say more? Now, I listen to my cravings and stop eating when I am full. I know my weaknesses. My body has a hard time digesting some foods. I love pure chocolate and my favourite fruits for a boost. My weight has remained the same since adulthood, and I returned back into shape after having a child. Unlike my mum, I am a spoon shape and 6'1".

Do you relate to either of us? Or are you someone with a different body story?

Please eat your fruit, vegetables, fibre sources, all of the good fats and oils and have some serious protein in some form, as well as calcium, zinc, sunlight and lots of water! Remember that you need fat to survive. A dietician, nutritionist or even your GP can guide you to the healthiest fat-weight ratio for you – make sure to take into account any allergies or genetic conditions that can affect you weight – and also be aware of and act upon the following common sense questions yourself: "Do I have trouble walking? Am I short of breath? Does my back hurt? How are my blood pressure and cholesterol levels?"

Being overweight causes health issues in some form or another, at some time or another.

Seriously, wouldn't you prefer the doc to say "You are fine!" instead of ignoring your body and being told "If only you had come in sooner?"

But most importantly, make sure you have a positive attitude. All of this nutrition in all its forms is important to a point, but a negative attitude is what ultimately has a tremendous impact on your health and appearance and depending on your genetic (un)awareness, any injuries or operations, what you eat and what you feel and think about yourself can send you off in the wrong direction entirely and affect your present and future body shape, image and self worth!

THE PRANCE

Skill #2: The Runway Of Life

"A runway coach is born" – J. Alexander – Author, 'Follow the Model' and Catwalk coach on America's Next top Model (1991 to present)

How you walk is the pinnacle of presence.

Think of someone you admire. For obvious reasons, some of us won't know the freedom of walking. I want to let you know you can be the pinnacle of presence even if you happen to arrive in a wheelchair or not able due to a disability or an illness.

Do they have a walk of their own? Are they noticed when they walk into a room?

Supermodels can earn the majority of their income from their walk, so if you ever need to walk on stage to receive an award, give a speech, enter a meeting or an interview, you are going to need to walk confidently so it works to your advantage.

Supermodel walking secrets:

* Shoulders – create a good direction and openness to improve breathing.

* Walking joints – ankle, knee and hips.

* Use your hips and walk freely with your own rhythm.

* Relax – work your core for back support and balance.

* Practise the high heel factor.

* Maintain a pace that suits your walking style and body shape.

What now?

We obviously start with bare feet. You need to be able to walk properly before you go any higher, and we must reactivate your core muscles.

As everyone walks differently, I'm going to briefly introduce a technique that was created by an

Australian actor 120 years ago and has been used by actors, models and thousands of others ever since. Introducing The Alexander Technique! We're going to use this technique for the specific purpose of walking properly.

There are three movable joints when you walk. These are your hips, knees and ankles. All need to move naturally, especially your hips.

Second, you need to engage your core or tummy muscles. Now, on some of you, these muscles may be hiding, but trust me, they are still there and would love nothing more than to help you walk properly. These core muscles hold your back, help maintain your centre of gravity and are where you achieve physical balance. (Your ears have another major part in these areas, but we're not going there today.)

Next, you are going to rise up onto your

toes. In this moment, you lose one of your movable joints being your ankle and, consequently, your body will reshuffle itself in order to walk and stop you from falling over! Now…you are up on your toes. Walk around, stopping every now and then to check your balance and breathing.

In high heels, or shoes with lifts for men, start by removing your shoes. If you can walk around in your toes, you can walk in high heels! So, high heels on, and walk...

Remember that because you have lost mobility of your ankle joints, you really need to use your hips to walk effortlessly and properly in high heels or taller men's shoes. This is where The Alexander Technique is a huge help. Let your hips move and swing naturally! All you need to do now is practise...practise...practise! You will feel your confidence increase when you are feeling more in control.

If the amazing Naomi Campbell can fall down in Vivienne Westwood skyscrapers mid-showing, then the rest of us have a chance. Your heel choice and height will change with you. Whatever you love wearing, wear it! As long as you are not shuffling along, hunched over in order to compensate for your new inches!

"Beauty is pain…sometimes. But don't you just *love* my shoes?!"

Spotting

Before you can turn effortlessly, you need to have a good idea about the spotting element. Spotting is used primarily by dancers and models when turning. Pick a still spot, object or mark in the direction of the turn you are heading. As you turn, your head is the last to move from looking at the chosen spot and as it spins around it refocuses on the spot or mark. Use this technique when you are turning 90 degrees or 180 degrees, and then, let your head drift controllably, because if you whip it around, you **will** fall over!

Catwalk Turn

If you want to know how to do a professional catwalk turn, then this is for you. Your feet are the obvious place to start and the use of our toes and core muscles are back! This is not a technical turn, but to do any turn, you need to again focus on your direction point and judge whether or not you need to keep your feet close together or you need to carefully "dance" around.

Try to keep your feet underneath you so you are not launching out and losing your balance. Practise in bare feet on different surfaces until you want to try adding shoes. Like walking, if you can maintain your balance and spotting technique, then you'll be turning beautifully in no time!

How to stand comfortably within a line!

I once got one of the best jobs I've ever had while I was standing in a taxi queue. So how do you stand…when waiting to be introduced? When waiting for a bus or taxi? When giving a speech or accepting an award?

The modelling stance, or "line" as it is referred to in the industry, is an easy position to learn and adapt to any of these possible situations. Place the right or left foot, whichever is most comfortable, in front of the other foot's **big toe joint** and turn the front foot out to the side. Now, your weight should be on the back foot, and the ball of the front foot is positioned near the toe joint. You would need to then literally jiggle your body to establish a comfortable standing position.

You may, or may not notice that this

position comes from the "rocking" that most of the models of my day used to do and seemed quite helpful when I was practicing to sort out my balance, ultimately creating a good line and comfortable standing position.

Depending on what you are doing and/or holding while you are standing beautifully, your arms and hands can be behind you, gentle crossed or half crossed.

Holding a napkin and glass in your left hand so you can meet and shake hands with your right hand is another option.

And not forgetting the boys...

There are four steps for a gentleman standing.

First, stand straight. Number two, keep your head up comfortable. You don't have to be an idiot about it. Yes, I grew up with three brothers and all of their friends. Third, place one foot slightly off to the side. Finally, swap your feet as is comfortable.

Again, depending on what you are doing and/or holding, your arms and hands can be neatly crossed at the front, or holding something in your left hand so as to have your right hand free to greet people and shake hands.

Gentlemen, try and avoid the seemingly innate response to stand with your hands clasped over your nether regions. We ladies would really appreciate it!

CAMERAS

"When it comes down to it I let them think what they want. If they care enough to bother with what I do, then I'm already better than them." – Ms. Marilyn Monroe

I have four words for you: "Social media. The End."

Being in front of the camera is commonplace today and I am personally loving the fact that because technology has made it easier to communicate and create global friendships, relationships, communities, businesses and causes, we also have the opportunity to reconnect visually with our audience through this platform. In fact, why aren't we producing more visual resumes and CVs for employment opportunities? Screen tests for everyone!

Which brings me to the skills required for

your confidence (presentation) when in front the camera. As I have earlier mentioned, a picture tells a thousand words and these pictures are available for **anyone** to see…**forever!**

So seeing as though you never know who is going to see these pictures of you, here are a couple of supermodel must-do's to make sure that even when the camera sneaks up on you (bloody paparazzi!), you have more of a chance of a great shot.

The eyes have it! You have a few choices here. Either open them up and stare into the camera like you are threatening death. Or you can pretend you don't see the camera and turn your head leaving your eyes to spy. Finally, close them Marilyn Monroe style and pray it looks good!

Know which side of your face (your profile) looks more appealing. The camera does add some unfair proportions at times. Having some idea and asking trusted, honest friends what looks better will be a blessing down the track. This is an image of you, who you are and what you like the world to see. Give the world who you <u>really </u>are and be proud of it.

SMILE! A smile comes from the heart and shows in your face and eyes, so even if you have crooked teeth or braces, everyone looks beautiful when they smile.

For whatever reason, we all have something about ourselves we don't like. I figure this is one of the cons of being part of the human race – how we were born gets painted, prodded, wax, buffed and injected to either look like someone else or believe we will be happier when we look in the mirror. So...if you're in front of the camera and you have gone to all of that effort, you may as well put all of your likable features in the forefront.

Supermodels, who you should remember are human beings and have their own flaws, know what works for them when in front of the camera. This takes a lot of practice, some constructive feedback and determination. Remember too that a model's main job when they are in front of the camera is to sell and influence.

Here are a few ways to become confident in front of the camera as well as help you get an idea what works for you. You will need someone you trust and whose opinion you respect, a phone or camera and some fashion magazines.

Step 1: Take a photo of either side of your face. We are after profile shots. Which side is your best? Play around with lighting, as this will make a huge difference. More on lighting in a minute.

Step 2: Look through some magazines and

pick a few different poses to copy. Pay close attention to hands, fingers, feet positions, shoulders, chin and eyes. Take a few shots of you copying the positions and compare with the magazine shoot. Try angle shots.

Step 3: Have your friend take some shots of you sitting down, standing, looking away from the camera, also from up high and lower than you. Play with different positions with your arms and feet. You may feel a little weird and out of your comfort zone. This is good! Every supermodel has felt this, some still do, but you will be surprised by how confident you will feel once you know what works for you.

Lighting

I also want to briefly mention the importance of ***good*** lighting when having your photo taken or when you are being filmed. While you are having your private photo shoot, experiment with different lighting types and styles. For example, the best or most flattering natural light is early in the morning or late in the afternoon. Direct light, if you are indoors, needs to be on both sides of you.

Watch for shadowing if light is behind, directly above or directly below you. Also depending on the type of skin type, skin colouring and chosen clothing (remember: mastering your body shape and image!), lighting can make you look washed out, ill, flushed, lobster-esque or, God forbid, dead!

Tips From A Professional Photographer

As told by Lauren Elizabeth Pirie Bath, Pirie Bath Photography

From a photographer's perspective, I like to see my model or subject very comfortable. To achieve this, I employ a variety of techniques to get the best shot. Not all photographers are as considerate as this, so I guess my top tip is to do your research in hiring a photographer and ask them how they capture beautiful portraits. If what they say resonates with you, then give them a chance.

My workflow is to just let the model sit and let them know I'm testing lighting and exposure. I regularly shoot portraits, so I then start with some easy poses like hands out front and crossed legs until I can see the angles that work well with my model. Once I have a pose I like, I make minor adjustments to the tilt of the face, hands and posture until I'm happy. Then, I move on to another pose. In that way, I am almost 100 percent in charge of the session and my model doesn't have to worry at all. I talk between takes and try to get people to relax and laugh then shoot off some candid shots too!

My **second tip** is if you have a good photographer already, listen to what they tell you. If they're not communicating properly or you don't understand, then just let them know. Never become frustrated or anxious if you don't get it right. This doesn't make for great portraits.

As **tip three**, always bring up concerns. If you think you're showing too much leg or being photographed from a bad angle, just speak up rather than walk away feeling unsatisfied.

Tip four is to try and be as natural as

possible. Easy to say, but sometimes hard to do. If you have a competent portrait photographer, this is what they'll be after, anyway. Have a chat, get to know them and try your best to relax and give in to the moments.

Tip number five is to keep your look pretty but low maintenance and easy to fix between shots. Bring a change or two of clothing for variety. Different clothes suit different environments and looks.

LOOKING FOR WORK

Skill #4: The "Casting" Interview

"Spend one year being a tiger, not 100 being a sheep!" –

Madonna

Don't worry if you haven't quite "got there" in some areas of this book, as you will always be learning, trying and experimenting, but trust me – you are a lot further along than you realise!

But what about your CV or resume? This is your "pitch-on-paper." How do you sell yourself without the person meeting you, seeing what you look like, how you communicate or if your personalities either get along or seriously collide?

Do you have a brilliant CV or resume that will grab the attention of a manager who would like to meet you and see if you are the right person for his business (either as a client or as an employee)?

WHAT TO INCLUDE IN YOUR CV or

RESUME

* Resume is a detailed document with a set format.

* CV is a 1-2 page summary with a basic format.

* Represents and markets you on paper.

* Describes your skills, strengths, knowledge, education, experience and interests.

* Needs to stand out to make the reader want to meet you for an interview.

Resume: Your resume is the full detail of your work experience, education, qualifications, any awards you may have received and these have a specific format shown in the online templates. You may include a photo unless specifically told not to. The employer will ask for either a resume or a CV in the advert, or if you have approached someone for an opportunity.

Curriculum Vitae (CV): This is the shorter, more condensed version and needs to be specific, get straight to the point and can be a little more personal. A CV can add you own style without blurring the information required.

It is always a good idea to add a brief introductory letter in front of your resume or CV. This shows professionalism, thought and organisation. It is also another opportunity to help you stand out from the other applicants. A template for an introductory letter is also attached.

* Try and do some research about the business you are applying to and this includes trying to find out the person the letter is to be addressed. So for example "Dear Manager..." can get lost in the pile and who knows what circumstances the manager may be busy with during the time of recruitment.

* Also, please note that there is a completely different style of application for any government related position. These applications normally require you to answer "selection criteria" and there is a specific way of doing this. The best idea would be to do some research on the internet or locate trained consultants who help complete government position responses. Also, picking the brains of anyone you know who has <u>successfully</u> applied for a government position could also be helpful.

* Be honest! There is nothing worse than over promising and under delivering.

* Double check your spelling and grammar, especially the company name, position description and the person (including their title) to whom the application is being addressed. Don't trust spell check!

* Only abbreviate your qualifications. Never

write VIC, QLD, IL, CA, etc.

* If you are unsure of the title of a female
manager or recipient, write Ms.

Example Cover Letter

About the examples…

The following letters are written as if in
Australia with addresses, but if you are located
anywhere in the world, the same format applies. All
you must do is swap out the address for your local
employment ventures.

If E-Mail

{Date}

{Company name as advertised}

Via E-mail: {e-mail address}

RE: Position #ozcare2420 {Re-write
however position is advertised}

To Whom It May Concern, {or title of
person resume is to be addressed – make sure

spelling is PERFECT!}

Thank you for the opportunity to apply for the above mentioned position.

The attached Curriculum Vitae {or resume} details my experience in a number of roles that I believe qualify me for this position.

Thank you for your time and I look forward to hearing from you in the near future.

Yours Sincerely,

{Signature}

{Your name}

Introductory Letter Example (Snail Mail)

9th September 2013

Attention: The Manager

ABC Electronics

23 Colby Court

Mount Nathan Queensland 4212

Hand Delivered {– remove if not able to

deliver by hand. Hand delivering can be an advantage as you can get the name of the receptionist for future follow-up calls and contact and he/she can mention your appearance and enthusiasm to the decision maker/Manager!}

RE: Fulltime Sales Position (The Bulletin, 7th September 2013)

Dear Mr Smith,

I am applying for the above mentioned position and have attached my resume for your review. I am able to start immediately, have my own transport and would appreciate the opportunity to meet with you at your convenience to further discuss the role and my experience.

If you have any questions, please do not hesitate to contact me anytime.

Thank you for your time and consideration and I look forward to hearing from you soon.

Yours sincerely,

Miss Jane Doe

Mobile: + (XX) XXX XXX XXX

CV Template

Curriculum Vitae of (full name)

Confidential

Personal Details:

Name:

Address:

E-mail:

Mobile:

Phone: ( )

Education:

(Date - Institution, State, Country)

For example: 2010 – present - Gold Coast Tafe, Queensland, Australia

(Detail)

For example: Successfully completed

Certificate II - Developing life skills through

modelling

(..And continue back to college or equivalent

(do not include primary school!)

Work Experience OR Employment

History:

(Date – Place of Employment, State,

Country)

For example: 2010 – present - ANZ Banking

Corporation, Queensland, Australia

(Detail)

For example: Describe what you did and try

and break it down to dot points and include detail

that is most relevant to the position you are

applying for.

(.. continue back about 10 years maximum)

Personal Attributes: This is where you can

mention skills and things you are good at when

dealing with other people and what others think of you. Also, mention attributes that you believe the viewer would be looking for in an applicant.

Achievements: Any awards and goals you have achieved.

Hobbies: What you like to do in your spare time either on your own, in a team or with family and friends.

References: Try and have three as a minimum and a combination of personal and professional references. Note: You cannot use your family members. Always ask the referee's permission to use them and feel free to give them a heads up about the position you are applying for and that they may get a phone call.

(Name – Mr, Mrs, Professor etc.)

(Personal/Professional)

(Contact) and (b/h – business hours) or (a/h

– after hours)

First Interview Advice

Let's go back to the time you may have applied for a position. This is still relevant if you have never applied for a position, you are about to go for your first interview or your 101st interview! You were asked to attend an interview, a casting or an audition.

Ask yourself...

Why did I apply for this position?

Why do I want to work for this person and/or organisation?

Where do I want to go in this field or vocation?

When am I able to start if offered the position?

What amount of money am I legally entitled to?

Always take into consideration all of your entitlements such as superannuation, medical, insurances, taxes, etc. that are applicable within your state or country and ask if these are included in the figure that was given to you OR on top of the figure that was given to you. You then have the opportunity to consider if you will be going home with a decent pay cheque or not!

What amount of money will help me get ahead?

Congratulations!

You've arrived. The day has come and you are likely to be one of many! It's **your** time, so use it to **your** best advantage.

Interviews are part of life, your career and future. Whether you are being interviewed or conducting an interview, this process is a great way to find out more about a person, company, business vision, further learning, training opportunities and, of course, how much someone is willing to pay you for your skills and knowledge.

Whether you have applied via a phone call, video Skype call, walked in off the street, e-mailed or posted your CV or resume to this lucky manager it has worked – interview request received. So what now? Well if you haven't screamed with excitement, disbelief and nerves – do so! The first part of your pitch has worked. Now you need to bring that resume or CV to life when you walk into the room, prepared, confident, receptive, nervous and curious.

The interview process almost always looks something like this (unless you going to work for Google and then anything could happen!)

First impressions count. This is your reputation on the line with this interview and every other one you may attend, so start doing some research about the organisation. Go for a wander past and even venture into the building to see how other people are dressed. What does the place feel like? For example, is the foyer warm and inviting? Energetic and fast paced? Or cold and depressing?

Look…through newspapers, online job sites, magazines, notice boards, shop windows, cold call in person and on the phone from the local phone directory, ask friends or create your own opportunity.

Resume or CV time:

* Apply exactly as advertised.

* Call the business and research to find the best person to send the resume or CV.

* Try to obtain any contact details for a further follow up.

* Check the spelling of all names, addresses

and the body of resume or CV.

* The resume or CV is the first impression on paper. It needs to make the receiver want to meet you.

Response to a granted interview:

* Via e-mail, respond as soon as possible with a thank you and looking forward to meeting them repeating, with a date, time and venue.

Via phone, repeat the e-mail steps.

Prior to the interview:

* Always have a few copies of your resume or CV available in a neat folder, just in case the interviewer has misplaced it or if you need to refer to it during the interview.

* Have a working pen and notepad or diary to take notes for questions or responses.

* Think about what type of interview you are going to and the impression you want to give.

* Dress appropriately, paying attention to every detail, including hair, personal hygiene and accessories.

* Be prepared and think again about time and transport, so as not to arrive rushed or late.

* Be aware of your posture, body language, presentation and attitude while waiting for the interview.

* Positive thoughts and relaxation techniques will help alleviate any stress or anxiety.

In the interview:

* DO shake the interviewer's hand confidently and make strong eye contact while saying "Good afternoon… or Good morning… or thank you for seeing me… or nice to meet you …"

* DO sit down straight and with confidence.

* DO have some spare CVs or resumes and place your resume or CV, notepad with the *working*

pen or diary in lap and smile.

* DO answers any questions honestly, confidently and speak correctly.

* DO be prepared to answer any questions, explain how you may have achieved a goal or fixed a problem in the past.

* DO discuss teamwork as well as your ability to work unsupervised and on your own.

* DO be flexible and available as you may even get be asked to participate in a role play or help out then and there!

* DON'T be rude to anyone as you never know who you are talking to. Even the cleaner talks to your future boss.

* DON'T be arrogant or pretentious. Save you super confidence for when you have the job.

* DON'T tell people how to do their job.

* DON'T lie about your experience or

qualifications.

Some questions you may want to ask during the interview:

* How many people have applied for this position?

* When would I be required to start?

* Is there a uniform or set dress code?

* Do you offer any training or personal development opportunities?

* What is the pay?

* Does that include superannuation? If so, deduct about 10 percent from the total annual pay. Look into the taxes and forced saving benefits in your country or state so you are aware of what you will be paid at the end of the week or month.

* Type of position – casual, part time, full time, contract? (If not specified in the advert.)

* Is there any travel involved in the role?

* Is there a travel, food, accommodation allowance?

* Would I be required to be on call and if so, how often and on weekends?

* Any shift work or night work?

* Is there a probationary or trial period? (Standard is normally three months.)

* Are there regular performance reviews, if so, how often?

* What is reviewed?

* Where can this position take me?

Work experience process and question:

* Politely approach the person you want to work for, either by phone or in person.

* Begin by thanking them for their time and ask if they would be prepared to or are in the position to have you work for them for a week?

* Mention you do not expect payment for

the experience.

* Mention you are really interested in their profession.

* Have your resume or CV with you, or send it to them immediately via the best way for them to receive it.

* Note their correct name spelling, phone number and e-mail address.

* Ask for a follow up time to discuss further and organise a day and time to start.

* When successful, be early every time, be helpful, listen and ask questions and always be polite.

* Once the work experience is over, discuss any opportunities they may know of and ask for a reference.

Once the interview is over:

* Always thank the interviewer for their

time.

    * If they want to see you again or say they will let you know, be prepared to write down the time frame – for example, two weeks – and follow up at that time for any feedback, suggestions and a conclusion.

    * Write down any notes that may be helpful in your next interview.

My Thoughts

In the past, I have turned up for interviews for one position and ended up sweeping floors, stacking shelves, answering the phone and operating the cash register, all before being hired for a position that was never actually advertised. I have even had positions created for me! It happens more often than you think.

There have also been **A LOT** of interviews where I knew I had all of the skills and experience for the position and didn't even get a look in! But, as deflating as that was for my confidence at the time, the position almost always ended up being something I would have hated and more importantly another position presented itself soon after which I loved. My point: never give up!

Here are a few things you should expect at an interview:

* The interview should start as close to the time specified time.

* Respectful treatment.

* Honest answers to all of your questions.

* A thorough overview of what the position is about and what is expected of you.

* The ability to ask for and receive any feedback or suggestions for improvement.

* Privacy and confidentiality.

* Notification if successful within a specified

amount of time.

* Notification if unsuccessful and given an honest reason/feedback (then revert to point 5.)

* Always remember that even though you are being interviewed, you're also in a position to interview your perspective client or employer.

* The right to ask questions that are of interest and/or important to you.

* Positive thoughts. The definition of luck is when preparation meets opportunity! Good luck!

PRESENTATION

Principles

"The better you feel the more in alignment you are with your desires." – Esther and Jerry Hicks - The teachings of Abraham

The Personal Presentation Principles (PPP) in this book refer to skincare, hair care, the world of makeup and nail care.

Guess what? If you think clean skin, fresh breath, clean teeth, healthy nails and hair and your makeup are just good personal presentation and grooming, well, think again!

They are your first impression toolkit and, unfortunately, how everyone perceives you to be or *not* to be before you open your mouth. All supermodels are drop dead gorgeous – with their make up on and their hair styled to within an inch of its life! But I would wager that you wouldn't even recognise most of them without their catwalk faces on.

One thing you will recognise is their personal presentation and hygiene is always "super" as this forms the basis of who they are and what they represent.

Like some of us, not all supermodels are healthy, but the majority of them aren't the way they are without some serious and continuous time and work! Their personal regime consists of things beyond your wildest expectations or assumptions. Plus, you need to remember that a number of supermodels are paid to wear the beautiful skin care, make up and latest hair trends.

So let's get into it…

Skin

SKIN CARE

Your skin is the largest organ of your body

and your protection from the elements. It is also the barometer of what's happening with you, inside and out.

Firstly, find out what type of skin you have. **Normal** skin looks radiant, never dry or oily, and always feels smooth. The pores are never large or clogged. You could also be **normal to oily** or **normal to dry**. **Dry** skin looks thin and papery, feels tight and dry, has fine pores and sometimes, the skin gets flaky. **Sensitive** skin has visible redness, feels dry and itchy, is easily irritated and if rosaceous, can be very painful. **Combination** skin looks normal with either dry or oily patches, can feel oily in the T-section, may suffer from breakouts, may feel dry on cheeks and is the most common skin type. **Oily** skin looks greasy, shiny and dull besides feeling greasy. The pores are large, and you often have breakouts.

All supermodels drink a HEAP of water! You need to keep your precious organs flushed out and your skin hydrated. Add some lemon to your first glass in the morning to get you started and keep it going as much as you can throughout the day and night.

At first, you will you be going to the loo A LOT as your body will not know what has hit it as the toxic tsunami starts to move! But after a week or two, a couple of litres will be absorbed in no time and you'll have more energy and happier skin!

Whether or not you are interested in knowing, some things that can affect your skin are:

* Over exposure to sun

* Excessive amounts of alcohol

* Stress

* Smoking

* Pollution

* Antibiotics

* Allergies

* Poor diet

* Harsh facial scrubs

* Incorrect facial treatments and peels

* Over-exfoliation

* Changes in hormone levels

* Severe burning

* Age

* Allergic reactions

* Environmental changes

* Health and safety issues such as occupational stress and dehydration

* Dramatic change in weight

We all deserve regular pampering and supermodels are fantastic at this. Regular skin cleansing and pampering (such as facials and massage) help to alleviate any issues, deep clean, replenish and most importantly, relax the skin. Like anything in life, you get what you pay for and so, unfortunately, some trial and error may be required to find yourself the best products. A <u>professional</u> and <u>qualified</u> skin care therapist may need to assist you in your new skin treatment.

Some products I would suggest you investigate and invest in are:

* Cleanser – either milk or gel, foaming or otherwise. This product needs to clean your skin and leave it feeling clean and fresh without feeling tight or dried out.

* Toner – used after you have cleansed and, as its name suggests, tones your skin, refreshes the skin, closes pores and prepares it for the moisturiser.

* Eye makeup remover – removes the war paint after a long day and with today's products you need one that is able to remove waterproof/smudge proof/crying proof/rain proof makeup while being gentle enough for the very thin and sensitive eye area.

   * Moisturiser (day and night) – with plenty of water going in, you need protection from what is happening on the out(side) and the choices could take an entire other book to describe!

   * Exfoliant – this product can also be found in many guises and is essential for removing dead skin from around all of the trouble spots and for increasing the blood circulation into feeding your face and creating more new skin cells.

   * Mask – the best excuse to take time out for yourself. This product is normally either plant based or clay based and is an extra deep clean for your skin (there are even whole body ones which are heaven!)

* Eye gel or cream – I wish I had started using this product in my late 20's instead of late 30's. Rejuvenates and calms the overexposed eye area while helping to minimise laugh lines (yes, that is how I got them and that is what I call them!).

* Pigmentation reducer – sun damage, aging, certain medications, hormones and the joyous and at times, relief giving contraceptive pill can cause pigmentation. This product can either be a cream or a serum and is available as an extra step in your routine if you are receiving treatment or just want something extra in your routine.

* Serum or concentrate – an extra kick or special treat for your skin which can cost the earth, can be too rich for some skin types, but with the smallest of drops needed, will last you quite some time and the improvements in your skin are seen quite quickly.

* Lip cream or gel – the skin is thin around the lips and this product has the same reasons for use and results as the eye gel or cream.

* Body scrub – an exfoliate for your body to be used prior to a full body mask (called a wrap in the spas) or before moisturising with your favourite moisturiser or body butter.

* Body butter or moisturiser – body butter is normally thicker than your standard moisturiser and normally has a base of cocoa or Shea butter. Depending on your skin type and amount of water you drink, one or the other will work better for you.

* Hand and nail cream – The most used product in your arsenal. You need to find a product that absorbs easily while keeping your hands hydrated and protected as well as keeping your cuticles moisturised and your nails strong.

Here is a step by step description of a basic skin

care routine for night and morning. No, I'm not trying to be funny, the reason why I have written night then morning is because your night routine is super important. It is hopefully followed by a long and restful night's sleep so your clean fresh skin has a chance to breathe, rejuvenate and do its best work while you are sleeping. So, **always cleanse right before you go to sleep** – night or day (this includes you lucky shift workers and all night partiers!).

Night Skincare routine

Your night skincare routine consists of mainly cleansing, toning and adding other creams that you might need that are particularly useful if applied at night. Also, depending on your skin type, once or twice a week you need to exfoliate and mask at least once a week.

Step 1: Begin by removing any makeup. Most cleansers have a makeup remover component, which makes it even easier because you can jump into the shower and do it all at once. It's a fantastic time saver. But if not, fill the sink with warm water and remove all your makeup, being careful around the eye area.

Step 2: Put a small amount of cleanser in your hand (depending on the product) and lather up the cleanser with some water between your hands for a little bit and then begin with circular motions on your cheeks going from the inside out.

With the same circular motions, move up your face and around the outside of the nostrils and out towards the ears and your jaw line. Continue to steadily massage in a circular motion and you could also do some zigzag motions using your index and middle finger of both hands, concentrating on your chin, above your lips and forehead area.

Steadily move up on either side of your nose,

the bridge of the nose and in between the eyebrows. This area is known as your T-zone. Giving this area a good clean, as it is prone to oil and dirt. Remember to be very careful around her eyes area with any type of product. Continue to massage your forehead and then rinse off all of the cleanser.

Step 3: Once or twice a week (depending on your skin type), you should follow your cleanse with an exfoliation. The secret of exfoliating is to make sure the grains are really small (avoid apricot kernels as an ingredient) and let the exfoliate do the work for you, so just lightly apply the product and gently massage all over the face.

Note: Some exfoliates are to be applied to a dry face before you cleanse and then are gently rubbed off until all the exfoliate and dead skin are removed. Only then rinse your face with warm water and make sure there are no granules around the side of the hairline and jawline.

Step 4: Again, depending on your skin type, you will need to apply a special treat for your skin – the mask. Apply the mask around are the nose area are definitely around the whole mouth area because you'd want to do a deep clean all over your face again being careful of the eye area and get into the crevices around to nostrils, over your nose and along your forehead.

My friend Terri Oldfield gave me a great tip for applying my clay mask. As my skin type is normal to dry, after cleansing and exfoliating, I should apply the mask in the shower before I wash my hair and all of the other shower rituals I perform, as the clay absorbs the steam from the shower, which means it doesn't dry the skin out and does an even better job of doing a deep clean. My pores are open and that's the time the mask needs to do its work. Rinse it off thoroughly with warm water, but also use a face cloth (which I prefer) to make sure you get all of the mask off.

Step 5: Once you are out of the shower or have been otherwise enjoying your mask, it's time to either spray toner on your face or some people prefer to spray a cotton face pad and then just lightly wipe over your face.

Step 6: Put enough night cream in your hands and gently moisturise your face and neck area. Then apply your eye cream, lip cream and/or your spot blemish gel if that's what's needed (which we all do need every now and then) and then you ready for a lovely night's slumber. Sweet dreams!

Morning Skincare routine

It's morning and if you're like me and a single mother, your child has woken you way before you're ready to get up! It's 6.30am and here we, "Go! Go! Go!"

Step 1: If you have a shower in the morning, then you just repeat what we did for night time, except the mask. Otherwise, get yourself in front of a sink of warm water and simply use a face cloth to rinse your face and get the blood moving. I personally do not cleanse in the morning as too much cleansing will strip the skin's surface and undo all the good from the night's sleep. Suffice to say, when I have been so exhausted (or drunk) to wash my face when I have got home that a cleanse, tone and a whole tub of moisturiser is required in a vain attempt to re-hydrate my poor skin!

Step 2: Tone.

Step 3: Moisturise. I do recommend investing in either a moisturiser with a sunscreen or a sunscreen that can be applied after you moisturise. Try to apply your moisturiser before you get on with organizing breakfast and your day so it has time to sink in before applying your makeup. Again, your skin type will dictate if you do need to apply anything else as part of your morning routine.

Remember to keep drinking up to eight decent sized glasses of water a day and take some time out to look after yourself, inside and out! Any effort is better than no effort at all. Keep track of your routine with a calendar.

Face

MAKEUP

This is *sooo* personal! I am a huge admirer of people wearing makeup daily and makeup that truly transforms and enhances their features.

After many years of wearing makeup firstly on stage in my ballet career, followed by my modelling career, I've been an "au natural" girl for a long time now, so when the makeup does come out,

I enjoy the experimentation with colours, styles and the covering of all of my deserved aging spots, sun damage, lines and blemishes.

Supermodels very rarely do their own makeup, but when they do, they too have watched the professionals and asked questions so they don't look like a Franken model when they leave the house!

I've consulted a number of model makeup artists, and here a couple of tips they highly recommend:

* Discover your face shape

* Is your skin a cool or warm tone?

* Test foundation on the back of your hand as this is the closest to your face.

* Make an appointment with a professional and qualified makeup artist and ask a lot of questions.

* Practice, experiment and have fun.

* Maintain your facial hair - especially your eyebrows (again, it's worth the money to have these professionally done, and then you can <u>carefully</u> pluck them to maintain between visits).

How to determine your face shape:

Stand in front of a mirror. You should be able to easily reach it from a standing position in front of it – you'll need to be able to draw on it without having to lean forward. Stand looking directly forward into the mirror, with your back straight, your head high, and your shoulders back. If you have bangs, pull them out of the way.

Trace the outline of your face. Using lipstick, a bar of soap, chalk, a dry erase marker, or some other non-permanent sketching tool, carefully trace the outline of your face in the mirror. Start from the bottom of your chin, proceed up the edge of your face on one side past your cheek bones, follow the curve of your hair line, go down the other side of your face, and end up back at your chin. Try to stay as still as possible while you do this. NOTE: Don't include your ears - just the edges of your face.

Judge your facial outline. Step back and look at the shape you've traced. Where is it widest? Is it tall or short? What shape are your jaw and forehead? Based on the answers to these questions, your face *should* fit in to one of the following categories:

SHAPES

Oblong: Your outline should roughly resemble a tall rectangle with rounded corners. Oblong faces have broad but even foreheads, cheekbones, and jaws.

Round: If your outline closely resembles a

circle, with wide cheekbones and a tapering jaw and forehead, you might have a round face.

Square: Your outline should not be tall but should be wide at all points, with a broad forehead, strong cheekbones, and an angular jaw.

Oval: The forehead should be slightly broad, with narrower cheekbones and a tapering jaw line.

Heart-shaped: These faces are characterised by a broad forehead, strong cheekbones, and a small chin.

Triangular: If your outline features a broad jaw but a small forehead, this might be the ticket.

Diamond: A diamond face differs from a round or oval face in that the cheekbones are significantly wider than the chin and forehead, which are both narrow.

Warm and cool skin tones – what's

yours?

Your skin tone is the colour, or hue, of your skin and is determined by the amount and type of melanin in your skin and the size and number of blood vessels that lie closest to the skin's surface. Skin colours vary greatly from person to person, although those within the same ethnic group tend to fall within a range of the same type of colour tone.

Additionally, getting a sun tan will deepen your skin's pigmentation, but it will not change your skin tone. In order to make the appropriate choices for cosmetics, hair colouring and clothing, you need to identify the tone of your skin.

There are different ways to determine skin tone. You may find your own by following these steps.

Wash your face with warm water and a facial cleanser. Your skin should be completely clean of make up and other impurities. Pat your skin dry with a towel. Do not use moisturizer or toner and avoid rubbing your skin with the towel, as the friction will bring a red flush to your face and make it harder to detect your most natural skin colour.

Wait 15 minutes. Allow some time for your face to recover from the temperate water and subsequent drying in order to let it reach its most natural state.

Stand in front of a mirror. Make sure you are in an area that is full of natural light, as shadows and/or florescent lighting can alter the appearance of your skin's colouring.

Choose one of the following methods to determine whether your skin tone is warm or cool:

Hold a piece of white paper to your face. Take note of your skin's tone in contrast to the white. If it looks yellow or golden, then you have a warm skin colour. If it looks pinkish, you have a cool tone.

Take turns holding gold foil, then silver foil, to your face to determine skin tone. Take note of the effect of the reflection on the look of your skin. The right foil will give you a healthy, glowing appearance. The wrong foil will make you appear grey and sickly. If the gold foil is right for you, then you have a warm skin tone. If the silver foil is right for you, your tone is cool.

Clean behind your ears thoroughly and have someone else pull your ear forward and look behind your ear in natural light. The behind-the-ear skin is pure in tone and a yellowish or pinkish hue should be readily identifiable. If your partner sees a yellow hue, then you have a warm skin tone. A pinkish tint signifies a cool tone.

Hold your wrists out and facing up under direct sunlight. If the blood vessels seem to be greenish in colour, then you are a warm tone. If they appear to have a bluish tint, then you are a cool skin tone.

For all of you makeup newbies, here is a list of suggested products and equipment to get you started in the supermodel world of makeup application!

PRODUCTS

Concealer: A concealer or colour corrector is a type of cosmetic that is used to mask dark circles, age spots, large pores, and other small blemishes visible on the skin. It is similar to foundation, but thicker and used to hide different pigments by blending the imperfection into the surrounding skin tone. It is normally applied after primer, but before foundation and used on the face.

Foundation: Foundation is a skin coloured cosmetic applied to the face to create an even, uniform colour to the complexion, to cover flaws, and, sometimes, to change the natural skin tone.

Primer: A cosmetic primer is a cream or lotion applied before another cosmetic to improve coverage and lengthen the amount of time the cosmetic lasts on the face. There are different kinds of cosmetic primers such as foundation primer, eyelid primer, lip primer, and mascara primer.

Eye shadow: A cosmetic that is applied on the eyelids and under the eyebrows. Eye shadow can be applied in a variety of ways depending upon the desired look. Typically application is done using sponges, fingers, and/or brushes. The most important aspect of applying eye shadow, and makeup in general, is blending well.

Blush: Rouge, also called blush or blusher

(UK), is a cosmetic typically used by women to redden the cheeks so as to provide a more youthful appearance, and to emphasize the cheekbones.

Eyebrow pencil: A cosmetic pencil for defining or accentuating the eyebrows.

Loose powder: Loose powder provides sheer, natural coverage to set makeup, soften colour and smooth the texture of the skin for an overall radiant complexion. Use to set foundations, wear alone or lightly layered over primers to enhance a natural complexion.

Eyeliner: Eyeliner is a cosmetic used to define the eyes. It is applied around the contours of the eye, along and above the edges of the eyelids where the eyelashes grow and is often applied just on the outer half of the eye.

Mascara: A cosmetic used to darken, colour, thicken, lengthen or define eyelashes.

Historically, it was (and still is) usually black, but now it also comes in many colours and tints. Mascara comes in three forms: liquid, cake and cream. It is available in tubes with wand applicators. Ingredients in mascara include water, wax thickeners, film-formers and preservatives.

Lip liner: Lip liner is a term to describe a cosmetic coloured pencil that is used to enhance and define the lips. It is designed to be used in conjunction with lipstick or other lip colour products.

Lipstick: a cosmetic for colouring the lips, usually in the form of a stick.

Lip gloss/balm: Lip gloss is a product used primarily to give lips a glossy lustre, and sometimes to add a subtle colour. It is distributed as a liquid or a soft solid (not to be confused with **lip balm**, which generally has medicinal or soothing purposes). The product is available in ranges of opacity from translucent to solid, and can have various frosted, glittered, glossy, and metallic finishes.

EQUIPMENT

* Brushes for lips, eyebrows and eyes

* Sponges for concealer, foundation and some compact powders

* Facial pads used mainly for cleaning

* Tweezers

* Eyelash curlers

* Cotton buds

* Makeup remover

Your Crowning Glory

HAIR CARE

We weren't all born with long, luscious, thick, silky hair. Then again, some of us were... My apologies if this is sounding like a sulk because I was born with thin, fine, dead straight hair with NO elasticity whatsoever. At 15, I attempted a spiral perm, which lasted for a total of six weeks! All bitching aside, my hair is healthy, dries quickly and teases brilliantly! It did, however, take more than my fair share of disasters to realise this.

Let's have a look at your hair type and what you need to do to keep it looking gorgeous and supermodel-esque. Hair types are fine, medium, curly, wavy, thick, straight and frizzy.

How to determine your hair type:

Take a quick shower like you normally would. Take your time, don't rush :)

Afterwards, towel dry your hair. Squeeze all of the excess water out but make sure that your hair is still damp.

Then, blow dry your hair. Make sure that this time your hair is completely dry.

Now look at your hair after the drying. Is it puffy? Is it straight and flat? Is it wavy? Is it curly and puffy?

If your hair is puffy, that means that your hair is thick. If your hair is straight and flat, your hair is thin. If it is wavy, it is semi-thick. And if it is curly and puffy, it is super thick!

Now you can make a new choice about your hair. Would you like it thin and not thick? Straight and not curly? Curly but not straight? Most hair salons offer a few hairstyles for different types of hair.

For example, if you want thick hair, you can ask for layers in your thin hair and you will get thick hair in no time! If you want thin hair, you can get it thinned out. If you want straight hair, they can give you a straightening treatment. Also, if you want curly hair, a perm is fine too. Or you can use a curling mousse that is found in most salons because they sell their own products.

Because you already know your face shape, you can look at the web to decide on some haircuts and styles that will beautifully frame your face. Like your skin, you need to find a <u>professional</u> and <u>qualified</u> hairdresser/stylist you can build a relationship with. Someone you can trust and has other solutions than to just cut all of your hair off! A good cut is essential to excellent hair care and yes, your self-esteem.

My hairdresser Ramon (who also spent over twenty years as the hairdresser to the stars like Darryl Hannah, Julia Roberts and Brad Pitt – in Beverly Hills, of course!) and creator of the amazing new revolution 360° hair extensions suggests these tips for beautiful supermodel hair, no matter what you were born with: "Grow it! Don't fry your follicles when you are colouring! Fake it until you make it! Trim it regularly – your hair will thank you!"

Basic Hair Care Products

Try not to get too overwhelmed by the number of hair care products available AND by what they promise… trial and error will be your saving grace and unfortunately a few home truths will be learnt along the way! I say this from decades of trying to get thicker hair, only to end up with dry, brittle lifeless hair "volumeised" to within an inch of its life. As a dear friend said to me after one of my disasters: "Get over it – hair grows!" My hair is healthy, shiny, long, strong. It is still fine and I'm cool with it.

Shampoo – Find one that you like, but change it up every now and then as your hair likes change. Wash when you feel it needs a wash and don't discount having a greasy day at least once a week. This natural oil is brilliant for your hair and I highly recommend brushing the oil through thoroughly followed by a tasteful up-do.

Dry-shampoo – I personally LOVE this stuff! …But not all the time. Follow the directions and enjoy the covering of greys, re-growth, the oily roots and the extra volume.

Conditioner – Again, find one that leaves your hair shiny, conditioned, but not too heavy. Unless you have VERY dry hair (roots to tip), concentrate the application on the middle section to the ends and always comb it through and leave in for a minute or two before thoroughly rinsing it out. This makes sure the conditioner has covered all of your hair evenly and the residue on the comb is all that's needed at the root area. This process also cuts down untangling time when your hair is drying.

Treatments – Too many to mention! From Henna masks to Moroccan Argan Oil, depending on your hair type, if you are recovering from a 6 month bleaching fest or your hormones have gone bat crap crazy - trial and error is the way forward, have fun and follow the directions. Try an limit your treatments to once a month, twice if directed by a professional.

Split end oils – Essential (in my humble fine haired opinion) between trims to help your hair grow.

Pre Heat treatments – It's not rocket science to deduce that daily blow drying/straightening/curling, etc., puts your hair through immense stress. Use what works for you and maybe cut back on the daily heat stress and enjoy your natural locks occasionally?

Mousse – This invention changed lives

forever. Whatever hair type you have, mousse can be used with confidence that you will get the desired result, have hair that still moves naturally (not stuck to your head like a newsreader helmet) and seems to last forever.

Jewels, Not Tools

NAIL CARE

As impractical as it is for most of us, you can still look after your nails and keep them healthy and looking beautiful even if you dig ditches, wash dogs, wash dishes or look after kids on a daily basis. (I'm sure there are even dirtier jobs out there, so this applies to you too!) Have you ever really thought about your nails, what your nails do and how they represent you? Your nails are used and seen when you meet people, write, type, speak and, my personal favourite, talk.

Do I really need to say that not only do

bitten and picked nails look disgusting, but it really does show your lack of self-respect and self-esteem (bitten nails are up the with worn out socks and shoes, trackies with elastic around the ankle and MC Hammer pants!). Your nails go through a lot and deserve to be looked after like the rest of you AND they don't need to be long to be jewels!

Some rules of *thumb* for maintenance:

Learn to file your nails from the left to middle and right to middle.

Crystal files are fantastic, are gentle on your nails and last for ages!

Keep them an even length - nails are like hair, regular trims keep them strong and healthy

Invest in some Silica (gel or capsules) to improve your nail, hair and skin health from the inside.

Invest in a professional manicure (hands)

and pedicure (feet) at least once in your lifetime (they are addictive!), watch and ask lots of questions so you can maintain at home.

Once you have finished painting your nails tidy them up with the a cuticle stick and some acetone free nail polish remover instead of a cotton bud.

For your reference a basic nail care routine goes like this:

* Remove nail polish using polish remover and cotton balls or pads.

* Cut nails to preferred even length.

* Soak in warm water.

* Exfoliate hand or foot.

* Dry and apply cuticle oil or cream.

* File nails to preferred shape with nail file. File from left to centre and right to centre.

* Use cuticle stick to gently push cuticles away

from nail.

* Carefully cut excess cuticle skin.

* Moisturise areas especially tops of hands, heels and cuticle area.

* Remove any oil from nail with polish remover.

* Buff the nail if not applying polish.

* Apply a base coat, colour then top coat using the technique provided.

* Allow to dry for at least ten to fifteen minutes.

* Do not blow on the nail, wave hands or use a hair dryer as this will not dry the nail any quicker.

Here is a step-by-step process for painting and tidying up:

Make sure the polish is not too thick and clumpy or too thin. Shake the bottle well. Apply enough polish to evenly cover one stroke in the middle of the nail and one on either side of the first stroke. Apply one base coat, two colour coats and one top coat. Pour a small amount of nail polish remover into the lid. Dip the cuticle stick into the remover and carefully remove any colour that is in the cuticle or finger area. Use as much remover as is needed. Do not use any cotton buds or cotton wool as the fibres may become attached to the wet nail polish.

Trial and Error

This is what is required to find out what works for you…at the moment! Yep, your skin, tastes and budget will change. Not to mention products are discontinued (very annoying!) and there is always something new coming onto the market as the next big thing. So keep at it until you find what works for you.

Compare Ingredients

Finding out what you are putting into/onto your

skin and body is a really good idea. My trial and error started when I was 15, so I do know what works, what to stay clear of and what might work for where my skin, tastes and budget are now. I recently had an experience where my favourite clay mask was going out of production (arghhh!), so I had a look at another much cheaper brand and surprise, surprise exactly the same ingredients and a third of the price (yayyy!).

To Save or Splurge?

Good question! My answer is to combine the top two paragraphs and definitely spoil yourself with a luxurious product when you can. I have tried A LOT of products to finally come down to a solution that suits my budget, requirements and daily routine. At the end of the day products are promoted as miracle cures to sell and make money – if they actually do what they say they can then that's an added bonus. Just remember we are all unique, so what works for someone else may not work for you … but you won't know until you try.

Of My Endorsement

A brand I love is The Mineral Goddess Range of Professional Mineral Makeup (kylies.com.au) – it is simply brilliant! The foundations are durable, safe and so easy to use. The mineral blends are 100% natural and pure, containing no fillers, preservatives, perfumes, colorants or parabens. This makes them perfect for sensitive and problem skin types and also great after cosmetic procedures. They can be used every day and are also fantastic for professional Makeup Artists to use for all their on-location jobs. It is perfect for weddings and special occasion makeup. It has superior coverage and is water resistant too. I know you will enjoy using these products as much as I do, whether it's professionally, as a makeup artist or on yourself.

Please be aware that as much as we all wish it were so, minerals are not a miracle cure for skin ailments and it would of course be unreasonable for anyone to make that claim. However, we have put together blends of the purest, medical-grade, natural minerals currently available that are free of any known irritants to help provide you with the looks you desire, with the least chance of an unpleasant reaction. If you do have a history of severe reactions to any skincare, hair care or other beauty or health products then it is advised that you first consult an allergy specialist for tests to determine the exact cause and/or offending element.

I am increasingly running into people who, proudly boast that their usual makeup is also Australian made. Unfortunately and unknown to them, they are mistaken! Sadly, several of

Australia's most popular makeup brands, once made here, are now very quietly being made in China and other low-cost/hi-risk countries. As a former big fan of the companies themselves and Australian made products in general, I am hugely disappointed with their decision.

My personal tips:

* Try to stick to a moisturiser that is easily absorbed for your face and body and try to avoid Sorbolene and Petroleum Jelly.

* Use non-acetone nail polish remover.

* Use Lucas's Papaw Ointment on your cuticles, lips and eyelids at night.

* Blemish/spot treatments – use tea tree oil (Save) or Kiehls Blue Herbal Spot Treatment (Splurge).

* Use dry shampoo for extra volume, cover greys, regrowth and excessive oil.

* Invest in a split ends or protein rich treatment for your hair.

LIVING IN THE WORK

WORLD

`Skill #6: Your Professional Self`

"Create your own style... let it be unique for yourself and yet identifiable for others" – Anna Wintour – Editor-in-chief of American Vogue and Artistic Director for Condé Nast (1975 – present)

Everyone can do this! There is no art, no mathematical compound and no magic wands - there are however, professional stylists if you're really lost, a host of websites and then there's your own sense of style.

Your professional self moves beyond what you wear, your nails, skin and hair. Professional presentation is about social etiquette, speech, attitude, confidence and body language. How's your 'body shape' degree going? You know what looks good, what makes you feel good, what you want

116

and don't want and some idea of your next step…

Still nothing? Okay, please join me for a chat in my Attitude Booth. Attitude goes hand-in-hand with confidence. It is made up from your specific feelings, beliefs and perceptions, so think of it as the base foundation. Your own unique essence and true conviction brings the gold rim to your professional self and approach.

You have a choice about how your attitude places you for your long-term goals, immediate wants and forthcoming opportunities. Your attitude will either open doors or slam them in your face. I firmly believe in always being who you are, but I also believe that a good understanding and application of appropriate social etiquette can make a huge difference to you professionally (and personally).

Pro's for **Professional** social etiquette

include your career, employment opportunities, an increase in contacts and your professional network, your rapport and reputation amongst your peers and colleagues and your ability to make a difference and instigate change.

Pro's for **Personal** social etiquette include changes everywhere, such as your understanding and accepting of who you are, what and who you know, a confrontation and ease in new situations and a personal growth as a human being with the advantages of choice and action.

If you think manners and etiquette schooling is old fashioned, then think again.

I once went to a networking breakfast at the Versace hotel on the Gold Coast, Australia and the guest speaker? Kirstie Clements, journalist, author, mother and former editor-in-chief of *Vogue Australia* for more than a decade until her infamous firing due to – well, no one really knows! This dismissal of Titanic proportions led to two best selling books, speaking engagements and a goal to bring manners and etiquette back into the workplace.

So, are manners and etiquette relevant in modern society? Well, do you like being treated with respect? Do you notice a rare gesture of kindness and consideration? Do you believe that you should treat others the way you wish to be treated?

Manners and etiquette will differentiate you from the pack. Understand and accept that you have to compete for that position and opportunity with everything you've got and if you are not successful (this time 'round), trust me you will be remembered and you will be able to sleep at night knowing that you were courteous, genuine, considerate, polite and attentive.

Here is some etiquette advice you may want to consider incorporating into your new successful life.

At the top of my list is a personal lesson of learning to shut my mouth and listen!! This took me a while to work out as I was so consumed on proving myself, gaining attention for what I knew and impatient as hell to get to the top as fast as I could. Never assume you know more and/or everything when with others because you never know <u>what</u> and more importantly <u>who,</u> the other people know! You will learn to become wary of those who talk too much, put their ego before you, the organisation and the long term benefit of all concerned.

Secondly, create and be comfortable with your Professional 'out-look' and its social application. For example:

* Presenting yourself with the kind of polish that can be taken seriously.

* Automatically expressing good manners and courtesy in public.

* Being comfortable around people.

* Helping people become comfortable around you.

* Becoming aware of your personal mannerisms and actions.

* Becoming aware of and express you intercultural competence and understanding.

Inter-cultural etiquette may include:

* Being aware of and understanding diverse cultures and traditions

* Asking the host or hostess if unsure of how to approach a particular person or of any customs one should be aware of.

* Some customs remain within Australia, but may be more pronounced when in the host city or country.

Japan and China:

* Bow at a lower level than the host or guest of honour and only bow after this person has bowed.

* Present your business card with two hands and a small bow, similar to offering a gift.

* Pointing is considered extremely rude.

* Do not make eye contact.

* Only shake hands if the host/hostess extends their hand first.

* Males are still dominant in most Japanese business negotiations, but this is changing.

* There is still a prominent hierarchy of management and it is rude to speak to a senior manager without first being introduced.

* Value and honour is part of Japanese culture and they do not like to "lose face" as this is seen as a form of shame on the family or organisation.

Europe:

* Present the host or hostess with a gift of flowers or wine.

* Always sit after the host or hostess has been seated.

* Salad is served after the main meal.

America:

* Salad is served before the main course.

Indigenous:

* Eye contact is considered rude.

* Introduce yourself to the elder and ask permission to join them and their community.

* Any potential embarrassment can mean shame for the family and their community or tribe.

Dining Etiquette

Without question, dining etiquette is always noticed. Do yourself a favour and learn how to twirl your spaghetti on a spoon with a fork, keep your elbows off the table, always taste your food before you ask for the salt and pepper, don't talk with your mouth full, chew with your mouth closed and no ashtrays means No smoking! But wait, there's more…

* Never point, clap, whistle or wave for a waiter.

* When you serve yourself you must eat everything.

* When someone else serves you, just eat what you can.

* Try to eat from the back of the fork, never from the side.

* Discuss things that you know something

about.

     * Try not to gossip or "bitch," as you never know who will hear you.

     * If you ask for service be prepared to pay for it.

     * Always offer to contribute to the bill when on a date.

     * If a time is specified, for example, 5 to 7 pm, do not overstay your welcome.

     * Never experiment on your guests.

     * Be aware of any allergies or special requirements.

     * When seated speak to the people on both sides of you.

     * Introduce people how they wish to be referred, for example Sir, Mr., Mrs., by their first name or last name.

     * If unsure about table manners, wait until

the host(s) have started.

* Remember which glass or bread plate is yours

* Remember that your liquids are on your right and your solids are on your left

* Place your napkin on your lap as soon as you are seated. Do not remove it until the meal is concluded and everyone has finished. Partially re-fold the napkin and place it on the plate.

* Knives are traditionally placed on the right side of the plate with the blade of the knife facing the plate and the fork should be on the left of the plate. Start from the outside and work toward the plate.

* Once the silver is picked up from the table it never touches the table again. Between bites, it is appropriate to rest a utensil across the side of the plate. Do not lay it on the table or prop it halfway

on the table and against the plate.

* Break bread into small bite size pieces: Do not butter a whole slice or piece of bread at once. Butter should be placed on the bread plate, and small amounts of butter should be spread on the bite size pieces as needed.

* Never lift your soup bowl to drink the final drops.

Etiquette Essentials

* Try not to fall for "fad" fashions.

* At a zebra crossing, always acknowledge the driver that stopped nicely.

* Do not begin eating until after everyone has been served (this is the general rule for six people or less).

* At large functions, wait until your table has been served or given permission by the host to begin eating.

* Be open to trying new cuisines. If you do not like what you have been given, quietly dispose of your mouthful in your napkin. Politely ask the waiter for a replacement meal.

* Try to avoid ordering messy foods that are difficult to eat. If you are interviewing for a job or trying to win a business deal, you do not want to be worrying about the stain on your tie or dress.

* If you accidentally burp or hiccup, just say "excuse me."

* Head for the rest rooms if you must remove something stuck between your teeth.

* Do not use a toothpick at the table.

* Don't gobble your food in a rush.

* Don't lick your fingers – always use a napkin.

* Be on time.

* Turn off your mobile phone or

communication device as your full attention should be on your dining companion(s)

* Don't order the most expensive item or the least expensive item on the menu when you are being entertained, go for something in the middle price range.

Social Media Netiquette

And then there's online etiquette (take a deep breath and let me know what you think of this?!) Social media etiquette and being professional online when you don't have the option of using your tone of voice or body language has the potential to become an unintentional disaster that is with you for the rest of your life! Gone are the days of actual privacy where if you didn't open your mouth, no-one was any the wiser and you had a second chance to get it right, make the impact, say what you wanted to say and how you wanted to say it! Not any more… For example:

   * In the workplace, use social media only as directed by the organisation or employer.

   * Be aware of Twitter 'trolls' and report any type of negative, offensive, bullying or damaging tweets.

   * Do not criticise or make personal comments that could jeopardise your reputation, promotion opportunities or career.

   * Be aware of sensitive issues such as discrimination, sexual harassment and privacy when using social media.

   * Be creative and remarkable.

   * Abide by the rules outlined by each social media platform.

   * Be smart and conscientious as you never know who will read your comments.

Body Language

You and Your Body Language

Your professional self also encompasses body language. Thousands of books have been written on this subject that involves the possibility to gauge someone's thoughts by their actions, which can improve overall communication levels and strategic processes.

Our thoughts invariably control our actions, but in some cases our body language can be displaying the complete opposite of our intentions. Above all, if you think professionally, you're likely to act and present in a professional manner (most of the time!).

#1 Strong eye contact

People who look to the sides a lot are nervous, lying, or distracted. However, if a person looks away from the speaker, it very well could be a comfort display or indicate submissiveness.

Looking askance generally means the person is distrustful or unconvinced.

If someone looks down at the floor a lot, they are probably shy or timid. People also tend to look down when they are upset, or trying to hide something emotional. People are often thinking and feeling unpleasant emotions when they are in the process of staring at the ground.

Sometimes looking down and away from the body can indicate shame or guilt. Just be certain to validate this feeling by reverting back to the topic a second time to validate the body language reading.

Some cultures believe that looking at someone in the eyes is a sign of disrespect, or is only done with intimate friends or family, so this could explain why someone is avoiding eye contact with you.

Dilated pupils mean that the person is

interested. Keep in mind, however, that many substances cause pupils to dilate, including alcohol, cocaine, amphetamines, MDMA, LSD and others, health causes or eye disorders. Don't mistake having a few drinks for attraction.

If their eyes seem focused far away, that usually indicates that a person is in deep thought or not listening.

#2 The Mirror

If someone mimics your body language this is a very genuine sign that they are trying to establish rapport with you. Try changing your body position here and there. If you find that they change their position similarly, they are mirroring.

#3 The Arm Argument

People with crossed arms are closing themselves to social influence. Though some people just cross their arms as a habit, it may indicate that the person is (slightly) reserved, uncomfortable with their appearance (self-conscious and trying to cover it), or just trying to hide something on their shirt. If their arms are crossed while their feet are shoulder width or wider apart, this is a position of toughness or authority.

Also be aware of their surroundings. If it's cold, or it might seem cold to them, they're probably just trying to stay warm.

If they are rubbing their hands together or somehow touching their own body, they might be comforting themselves (which means they aren't enjoying the current situation).

If someone rests their arms behind their neck or head, they are open to what is being discussed or just laid back in general.

If their hands are on their hips, they might be waiting, impatient or just tired.

If their hands are closed or clenched, they may be irritated, angry, or nervous.

#4 Nervous?

If someone brushes their hair back with their fingers, this may be preening, a common gesture if the person likes you, or their thoughts about something conflict with yours. They might not voice this. If you see raised eyebrows during this time, you can be pretty sure that they disagree with you.

If the person wears glasses and is constantly pushing them up onto their nose again, with a slight frown, that may also indicate they disagree with what you are saying. Look to make sure they push up their glasses with intent, not casually adjusting them. Look for pushing on the rim with two fingers, or an extra motion of wiggling the side of their glasses. The frown or raised eyebrows should tip you off. (Note: A frown may also indicate eye strain, and constant readjusting of glasses could be the result of an improper fit. The distinguishing feature is whether they are looking directly at you while doing it.)

Lowered eyebrows and squinted eyes illustrate an attempt at understanding what is being said or going on. It's usually from a skeptical point of view. This is presuming they are not trying to observe something that's far away.

#5 Foot Fetish

A fast tapping, shifting of weight, laughing, or movement of the foot will most often mean that the person is impatient, excited, nervous, scared, or intimidated.

The meaning of feet tapping can usually be discerned depending on the context; if you are currently talking and they are tapping their feet, that is an indication of a desire to leave (though usually this behaviour manifests when the person is anxious to get somewhere specific, such as a meeting, rather than because of what you're doing specifically). Slow shuffling indicates boredom with the current situation. If during flirtation your legs/feet touch, tapping can generally be interpreted as nervous excitement. This is because if they were uncomfortable, they would discreetly move away from the contact, a much more subtle escape than indirectly trying to tell you to move away.

Note though that some people with ADHD will constantly jiggle their legs. It doesn't mean anything, it's entirely subconscious and, while eccentric, it is difficult to stop. Some people also do it out of habit.

If the person is sitting, feet crossed at the ankles means they're generally at ease.

If while standing, a person seems to always keep their feet very close together, it probably means they are trying to be 'proper' in some way.

Sometimes feet together means that they are feeling more submissive or passive.

If they purposely touch their feet to yours, they are flirting!

Some people may point their feet to the direction of where they want to go or sometimes their interest. So if it's pointing at you, he/she may be interested in you.

#6 Networking

Smart business people understand the value of networking.

Do you know why you need to network? Put simply, expanding your contacts improves your chances to build good relationships, generate referrals and increase your opportunities. Plus, the more people that get to know you – in different industries at different functions – the easier it will be for you to find the best sources when you need specialised information or the insights of an experienced professional.

Building relationships, meeting new people and getting involved is essential to creating and discovering the opportunities available for you. Walking into a room full of strangers is daunting, even terrifying for some people, but let me tell you from personal experience – you need to do it! You deserve to be there as much as the rest of them and they need what you have to offer. More than half of your business will come from referrals…. And again, you never know who you will meet that may be the person or offer to introduce you to someone who will change give you a go, recommend you and change your life forever. Add this to the fact that

9/10 networking functions have free food and beverages and you have a win-win scenario.

Here are some known ways to widen your circle of contacts by improving your networking strategy.

* Offer to help others. End meetings and calls with "Is there anything I can do to help you?"

* Communicate your unique knowledge and expertise to others.

* Share your own personal contacts tactfully and respectfully.

* Write personal thank you notes to people who help you.

* Always follow through on your commitments.

It works both ways – each of us has something to offer, and we can benefit other attendees by offering information, advice, leads and ideas. Let's say you have received an invitation to an event or its time for you to host a function. Does your mouth go dry and palms sweat at the thought of standing in a room full of strangers and not knowing what to say? It's certainly the way a lot of people feel when faced with the prospect of meeting and greeting strangers. However, it can also be one of the best business and social opportunities.

Some networking benefits include:

* Sources for new business.

* Affiliation or partnership opportunities.

* Meet competitors.

* Introduction or referral for job placement.

* Career advancement.

* Feeling better about yourself.

* Meet new people and invaluable business contacts.

* Promote yourself and your organisation.

* Learn new work practices.

* Hear from guest speakers.

* Visit new places.

* Making other people feel more comfortable which makes them want to know you and possibly do business with you.

So what is working a room? It's basically the ability to circulate comfortably and graciously through a gathering of people – there's nothing manipulative or calculating about it! If you really care about people and your warmth and openness are genuine, the professional benefits will always appear.

Body Language Basics

Plan your presence! Have a positive attitude. Focus on the benefits. Plan and practise your self-introduction (just in case you are not introduced), prepare your small talk and handshake, listen actively but not passively, be present and respectful by giving your undivided attention and know, if possible, who will be attending. Arrive early, dressed appropriately, with many business cards in tow. Make an effort! Remember, practise makes perfect.

Generally, the networking process can go like this: Carefully prepare your first impression as you are representing yourself and your organisation. Arrive within the designated time and thank the host for the invite and ask if there is anyone they suggest you meet. Introduce yourself politely, but have prepared questions to "break the ice" and start a conversation. Excuse yourself politely, and meet some new people. Ask for business cards, and ask permission to contact them in the future. Thank the host and leave within the designated time.

Stuck for an opening question or

comment? The best opening line of all may be a smile and a friendly "hello," but if you're looking for something a little more original, some good areas to comment on are the venue, food, organisation or the guest of honour/guest speaker.

Now that you have some opening ideas all you need is someone to test them out on! And the best part is you can always approach someone looking as lost you feel – they will usually welcome your conversation and you can help them out by introducing others to your conversation and encouraging them to network.

* Here are some tips on how to go about introducing yourself and creating a conversation:

* Present a statement that can be upbeat or an unusual observation.

* Ask a question that is relevant and open-ended (i.e.; How? Why? When? Where? Who?).

* Be polite and wait until someone has finished talking or eating and then introduce yourself.

* Make eye contact and smile to everyone you meet.

* Remember your social and inter-cultural etiquette.

* If someone is by themselves, introduce yourself and make them feel welcome. Introduce them to others if appropriate.

* Ask what people do and show some interest.

* LISTEN intently and let people speak without interrupting.

* Ask if they have been there before or if they use the host business' service or product.

* Ask for their business card and make a mental note about what was discussed.

* If you are new to the area, ask about local attractions, good restaurants, bars, etc.

* If you do not yet have a business card, say they are being printed and ask for their business card.

* If you smoke, try to wait until the event is over, unless you are invited by the host to join them, then it is your choice.

* If you have forgotten someone's name or title, be honest and say, "I'm terribly sorry. I have forgotten your name."

* Introduce the guest of honour or any overseas delegates to your guests. Make sure they have everything they need and are comfortable.

When approaching a group be aware that there is a difference between including yourself and intruding. Avoid approaching 2 people who look as though they are having an intense conversation.

Approach groups of 3 or more and only give facial feedback to comments. Be open to others who want to get in.

Now, you've had a great conversation but how do you move on? Most of us (with a conscience and a decent amount of integrity!), worry that its rude to end a conversation, but remember that the whole aim of attending a networking function is to circulate and meet as many people as possible. It's as simple as saying "Please excuse me, it has been lovely talking to you" and move to another part of the room – this reinforces the fact that you actually had someone else to see and you didn't leave because you were bored.

Three common networking mistakes (if you remember these you will not only be remembered BUT you'll be invited back!):

Mistake # 1: Getting drunk and/or abusive.

Do I need to expand on why this is a mistake?

Mistake # 2: Over staying your welcome. Everyone has a "use by" date and you want to be invited back!

Mistake # 3: Immediately launching into the "hard sell." Do you like being sold to before you get to know someone? Develop trust and rapport first.

Following Up

Now for the follow-up process. This is SOOOOO important and will definitely differentiate you from the rest of the 'free-food-hire-a-crowd'. Trust me! Think of it as you have met someone, hit it off and you would like to contact or see them again… professionally speaking you would:

Write down details about people to be followed up including their name, title, where you met, the date you met, the event name or host, conversation points you heard, ideas, mutual people of interest, a date to follow up, the method you will follow up (phone, e-mail, letter…) and points you will discuss.

Follow up with this person on the due date and repeat the process. You can enter your information onto a basic Excel spreadsheet or Word document. Always keep in contact with the person, becoming aware of changes in companies, personnel, management or a location that be of use at the next follow up. Never over contact the person. Once to twice a month is perfectly acceptable and shows your consistency, interest and professional commitment.

Follow-up Telephone Techniques

#1 Attitude.

Your mental attitude is very important when

using the telephone. You should set out that the contact is going to become a client, an affiliate or a friend. Keeping this mental picture clearly in your mind will help you to project the right image and achieve your objective, whether that be a follow-up meeting, an introduction to another opportunity, to gain an interview etc.

#2 The use of your voice.

If you were the contact being phoned, imagine what picture comes into your mind when you pick up the phone and hear an unfamiliar voice – that of a stranger or someone you don't remember meeting. If the voice sounds hesitant and cautious or meek and timid, you may not be too interested in meeting this person and you are certainly very conscious of your time and what this person can do for you. Consider also if the voice sounds like they are reading from a prepared script, then you might picture a recorded message and your response may be similar. However, if the voice is positive and friendly as well as confident and businesslike then you may be more inclined to talk to that person, maybe even meet them and hear what they had to say.

Try to speak with a confident, enthusiastic and positive tome in your voice.

How? Prepare yourself – learn and practise a type of script that you can have in front of you to refer to. In some cases having written what you want to say as a prompt can only add to your confidence.

Stand or sit upright. Good posture promotes clear speech and a positive attitude. If you lounge casually against the back of your chair, your voice and attitude may come across as being casual and try to avoid, chewing, drinking or smoking while on the phone – remember being present? Well it applies when you are on the phone as well!

Speak as though the person is sitting across the desk from you – trust me this works.

Smile as you dial. Remember the phone does not give you the advantage of eye to eye contact or the ability to read body language, so your personality has to be projected by your voice alone. A smile on your face does put a smile in your voice.

Make certain you will not be interrupted and take notes for the next possible follow-up call.

#3 "What if?"

Just to give you a heads-up, for whatever reason, the follow-up call may be met with some negativity, a momentary lapse of memory or just plain rudeness, so here are some responses for dealing with telephone objections (only to be used if you feel that there is some definite mutual benefit is creating this relationship or it's a bet!)

Response 1: "Fine, you have just said you are not interested, interested in what?" Making money? New ideas? Inflation? Getting the best value for your money? I'm sure they interest you, don't they?

Response 2: "Do you know exactly what you are interested in?"

Response 3: " Surely (insert name), if there were one or two new ideas on (whatever is the main interest of the person you are calling) that may be of benefit to you, I'm sure you would like to be made aware of them, wouldn't you?"

Response 4: "When people say they are not interested, I normally find that they either haven't any money or any time – which is it for you?"

WHAT'S A "SWOT?"

"Be yourself, because everyone else is taken." – Oscar Wilde

via Caroline Buchanan – World BMX champion and

Australian Olympian

Without a doubt, every model knows what they want. This is the first skill you need to be pretty clear on before the lippy goes on and you head out the door today and everyday from now on. You need to <u>know</u> what you want which is normally a result of knowing what you <u>don't</u> want to really become pressured to <u>get</u> what you truly want and <u>why</u> you want it.

Sounds easy enough? If you were asked without warning, could you answer with clarity and conviction?

There exist amongst us scientifically proven universal laws that answer our thought and wants,

154

that is, your vibrational or energetic and emotional alignment. You receive what you positively and/or negatively think about and believe you can have or will happen.

After you have finished reading this book there are some other best-sellers that go into more detail about your rightful inheritance of well-being which includes abundance, prosperity, excellent health, brilliant and fulfilling careers, true love and fully open psychic abilities. A list of these are available at the back of this book as I have read them all and are continuing to study and apply what I have learnt to what I want and why I want it.

So how does this relate to the modelling industry? Models have to know who to talk to and how to impress the influencers to ultimately get what they want - the job, the money, the fame, the travel, the contacts and the career.

Modelling and its associated industries have to be some of the most competitive and short-term careers one is lucky enough to sample.

Try this: grab a piece of paper and draw a line down the middle.

Write your likes and dislikes down either side of the line - just to get clear.

For example, do you like to get up early? Are you prepared to study? Do you like animals, hell, children? Are you a vegetarian or vegan? What likes and dislikes have your past decisions and choices unveiled in your current situations?

I can remember being asked to do my first SWOT analysis when I became part of the 'Power' suit wearing corporate fraternity as a Personal Assistant (PA) in the early 90's.

"A what?"

"A SWOT!"

Sounded like I had missed the memo to study up for this analysis, but it turned out to be an extremely beneficial exercise and to this day, I have used this process both on my own and as part of a team.

Examining your true **S**trengths, **W**eaknesses, **O**pportunities and **T**hreats is a fantastic starting block to brainstorm ideas and get some real clarity of what you really want and why you really want it.

The Rules

SWOT Rules:

1. Be completely honest with yourself while also allowing yourself the benefit of improvement.

2. This is a constructive exercise NOT a destructive one!

3. Anything is relevant including

practical, emotional, physical, spiritual and mental.

4. It is just a good idea to separate your personal from your professional.

Make a list!

Here is a list of questions you can ask yourself to get started and there is also an example of my own if that helps.

* What are my strengths?

* How do I relate to people?

* What do other people say are my strengths?

* What do I like to do?

* What can I not stand?

* What am I afraid of?

* What have my past work and life experiences taught me?

* Where do I see myself in 5 years time?

* What opportunities are available for me right now?

* What are my weaknesses?

* Do I like to get up early?

* Do I do my best work late at night?

* Am I good with numbers?

* Am I good with money?

* What are some potential threats to my industry or career of choice?

* Who are my competitors?

* Do I like the outdoors?

* What languages do I speak?

* Do I like children or to travel?

* Am I willing to keep studying and learning more?

* Where can this job/career lead me?

* Do I like cooking or computers?

* Can my weaknesses be overcome with

training and experience?

    * Do I like helping animals?

    * Do I volunteer or work for a charity?

    * What do I need to work on?

    * Am I a self starter?

    * Do I follow trends?

What does an example look like?

To give you an idea, I made four lists on a notebook page: My Opportunities, My Threats, My Strengths, and My Weaknesses. You could make a page for each list, divide the paper into halves, or make a square diagram. Our fictional person filled out the lists as follows:

My Strengths: "Great with people. Good listener and communicator. Like to include others. Value others' opinions. Champion the underdog! Intuitive. Healthy. Creative. Driven. Committed. Value my time. Learn from my mistakes."

My Weaknesses: "Impatient. Don't like to work late at night or on Sundays. Tend to get bored easily."

My Opportunities: "Decades of massive opportunity. Improvements in technology. Global development. Network and contact base JV and partnerships. Media attention. Competitor recognition. Client collaboration. Exit strategy realised. Millions of lives changed."

My Threats: "Stretch myself too thin – this affected my health. Early buy out/takeover without reaching full potential. Work/life balance as building business."

If you find yourself a little mentally exhausted after this exercise – good! If not, keep going! Now, look at your weaknesses and threats… Be creative and think about how you could describe these as strengths and opportunities respectively.

How Does It Help Me?

Now, this next part is where this first skill really gets going and so you don't have the chance to even begin with "I don't know what I want!", I have done some research on some other vocations associated with the modelling industry that you may be interested in researching further, or God forbid, actually attempting... who knows you might be REALLY good at it! As an added bonus (and after a request from a reader) I subsequently interviewed a wide range of successful men and women who worked out what they wanted and have done brilliantly in these vocations. They were incredibly approachable, inspiring and more than happy to offer their advice to help you.

ACTING

Pick your favourite actor – Australian or

otherwise. What a life! And what an amazing craft! An actor or actress' goal is ultimately about entertainment, inspiration and luring the audience into a character they are portraying and the story they are trying to tell. Actors often research the role they are to play including background information, historical detail, real life examples, interviews and physical resemblances that will allow them to be fully submersed within the character.

Depending on the production, the workplace can be varied - actors perform on stage, on television and in film. Consequently actors need to be flexible and able to adapt to their environment in order to be successful and in demand – employed. Other qualities actors need, are:

* Determination and a positive attitude.

* A genuine love for the arts.

* Dedication (there will be lots of auditions!).

* Some professional and ongoing training.

* Skills in dramatic performance.

* The ability to fully appreciate and understand the emotion, thought processes and feelings of the role.

ADVERTISING

What a world! What a game! There is a science to this profession as the main aim of this collective group of creators is awareness and sales. For you, as an individual, there are two key people I will describe.

The first person is the Account Executive (AE). This person's role is to maintain the relationship between the agency (their employer) and the client (the person/organisation who pays the bills!) The AE has to liaise between the client and the creative team to make sure that all of the client's goals and ideal outcomes are met. Additionally, the

AE manages the 'pitches' or ideas to the client, the client's advertising budget and normally has up to four non-competing clients to manage at one time.

There are a number of qualifications to get you in the game including a Bachelor degree, but overall the skills needed to do this job come from applying for an internship and learning on the job.

AEs need the following attributes:

* Excellent people skills.

* Excellent communication and time management skills.

* Well organised.

* Professional appearance and personality.

* Able to work long hours and stick to deadlines.

* Able to travel to clients if required.

* Able to handle pressure.

* Possess strong leadership skills.

A typical day for an AE may look like this: Check on the status of their client's present project with the creative department, including the completion time. Contact the client with an update and to discuss upcoming projects. Initiate any new jobs and changes of a behalf the client. Present and review any layouts, concepts and copy with the client for approval. Communicate any feedback from the client with the creative team and discuss the next steps in the campaign.

Remember the AE purely manages the relationship between the client and agency and is not part of the creative team - you do not create any designs or copy.

ARTIST

Being an artist means being a creator - plain and simple! Art, like beauty, is definitely in the eye of the beholder, so whether you paint, sculpt, draw, create music, carve, construct installations, dance or take photographs you are an artist.

Most artists do not create because it makes them rich - they create because they LOVE what they do. Now if someone rich or famous loves what you do... well that's another story!

Artists have a freedom that allows them to invent new techniques, see things differently and create their own style.

An artist tries to evoke feelings within the viewer and achieve a powerful response - any kind of response. Art is about sharing your unique message with the world, getting fully immersed in your world and having a lot of fun with your creative license. An artist's world is where mistakes are accepted, boundaries are stretched and interpretation shared.

BEAUTY THERAPIST (includes

beautician, massage therapist and skin care therapist)

A beauty therapist is the person you seek out to make you <u>feel</u> beautiful again. This involves any number of fabulous treatments from your head to your toes including facials, body treatments, manicures (hands), pedicures (feet), spa treatments, massage, body wraps and peels.

As a beauty therapist you have got to love what you do as the shows in your presentation, rapport and technique. A good therapist will do the job, respect your privacy and maybe even sell you a product or two - but a great therapist is someone you instantly trust, someone who listens to what you are concerned about, is professional yet personable, overindulges you and leaves you with such an amazing feeling of serenity, relaxation and indulgence, that she or he will be with you for life -

and you will happily pay for their services, advice and products.

A beauty therapist needs to be:

* Qualified and continuously learning new techniques and about updated services being offered.

* Professional and willing to earn your client's trust.

* Healthy and strong to work long hours.

* Knowledgeable and love what you do.

* Able to provide quality customer service from the first "hello" to the "see you in four weeks time" closer.

Your options as a qualified beauty therapist are:

* Be employed by a spa or salon.

* Lease a chair or room as an added service in another business such as a hair salon.

* Open your own business.

CHOREOGRAPHER

As a choreographer you have the amazing freedom that comes with the teaching and directing your clients/students on how to tell your story through their movements, steps and own rhythm to an audience, with the added bonus of having an audience see your work and feel the passion behind it.

Choreographers are generally people who have danced their whole lives and who love to create. Choreographers can work in a number of fields including dance, theatre, gymnastics, fashion shows, art displays, film, skating routines, music and anywhere a visual performance is present and they can work all over the world! They are able to work with solar artists, a couple or a large group of performers. They help build confidence, refine coordination, develop technique, provide entertainment and enhance performance.

Most importantly, choreographers need to have a keen sense of who they are is an artist and also what the target audience needs and wants to see. Basic skills of a choreographer are:

* Discipline.

* Determination.

* Appropriate qualifications and/or experience.

* Confidence.

* Creativity.

* Patience.

* Be an entertainer.

* Excellent communicator.

* Flexibility and the ability to "think outside the square."

DJ

The music for all the high end fashion shows in Australia, Milan, Paris, Brazil, Spain, London and New York have got to come from somewhere ...enter the DJ – the coolest job on the planet! It is also the only job in the world that I know of (based on my past serious clubbing days), that if you were born a lot less genetically blessed than the rest of the population, it didn't matter! Because once you got up behind those decks and put on those oversized earphones - honey, everyone wanted to sleep with you!

But actually playing music is not as easy as you would think. It takes skill and bit of natural talent to be a good DJ, let alone a great DJ. Anything that makes people dance, smile, trance and have a great time is a top vocation my books AND the girls are on par with the boys (Bexta, DJ Havana Brown and DJ Dakota very talented ladies and in demand all over the world). They love what they do and they go above and beyond to give their fans/audience an amazing experience and a good time.

According to a 2012 study[1] there are approximately 1.25 million professional DJs in the world so it's a fairly competitive game as well - and for the record, these include radio DJs, rappers and music producers. If this is something that interests you go out and give it a go – and please drop me a line and let me know your new tracks as I'm always keen for a new sound!

EVENT MANAGEMENT

Delivering the 'wow' factor is never more at the forefront than it is with this vocation ... you get to create something really amazing from nothing. Event management combines an idea or concept, project management and the development of events.

These events can be festivals, concerts, fashion shows, business openings, conferences and meetings, launches, after-parties, art installations or exhibitions and sporting events. If you have an idea, an event can be created for or around it.

Event management involves a number of key needs in order to create a spectacular and influential event. You need to combine logistics (the number and availability of female toilets at an event is almost always the first thing on any event manager's list!), identifying the brand or message you want to convey, your target audience (the people who will help you spread your message further), partnerships, sponsorship opportunities, technical logistics (sound, air-conditioning/heating and lighting), costings, refreshments, legal/insurance liabilities, media etc. etc.

On the flip side of the actual launching of

the event, the follow up procedures and reporting requirements are just as important in order to know what didn't work, what was a huge success and how much interest and money was generated.

You need to be in your element dealing with hundreds of things at once in order to survive and excel in this multidimensional vocation. And from my own experience - it's hard work BUT also a huge amount of fun and a very satisfying career choice!

Another aspect worth mentioning is sustainable event management. This is no longer some ad hoc wording primarily used in brochures to keep the 'greenies' at bay. This event management process is becoming increasingly important to your target audience and is the process used to produce an event with environmental, economic or social issues.

Social and environment factors are taken into consideration and implemented throughout the planning, organisation and hosting of an event by the entire team from manager and clients through to the sub-contractor, suppliers and venue.

There are a number of qualifications available from diplomas to degrees and beyond. The choices for employment as an event manager can be in the hotel, travel and hospitality industries, within IT companies, advertising agencies, public relations firms, corporations, news, media, non-profit organisations or as an event management consultant.

FASHION DESIGNER

I'm in complete and utter awe of fashion designers. From the masters down to the backyard T-shirt printers, they are a force to be reckoned with and put their ideas and passion on the line every day hoping that they will trend, sell and see people wearing their creations.

They study trends and sketch the initial clothing or accessory design (so if you can draw, you are already well on your way!) and they oversee the entire production, from concept to final production.

Luckily, there are some pretty amazing and supportive platforms for new designers to show (and hopefully sell) their designs, create a following and a trend and dress some of the best marketers for their designs: celebrities!

The nature of the industry varies for each designer. Some designers are employed by manufacturing firms and work fairly regular hours. This is a great way to get experience, but quite often the designer's creativity can be stifled and even overshadowed by the cost involved in delivery.

Freelance designers have all the creative freedom they could want, but are left with some seriously long hours and stressful situations.

Gaining a qualification in fashion design is a great first step, followed by an internship with the fashion house to gain experience in production, the background of fashion design, understanding the fit and aesthetics of their designs for specific clients and how to meet consumer demand. It is also highly recommended to gain experience in other areas of fashion, such as the retail industry.

You need to go into this career with your eyes wide open and be prepared to work hard, multitask, build relationships, try new angles, market and sell, sell, sell! Be bold, be brave and enjoy the ride!

FASHION STYLIST

Are you one of those people who has an

innate sense of style? Can you instantly pick what colours, patterns, styles and cuts would look good on others? Are you really good at making people feel at ease? My friend, you are at cupboard fashion stylist! And you could be part of one of the most popular emerging professions in the fashion world globally!

You could have a career selecting and accessorising for published editorial features, print or TV advertising campaigns, music videos, concert performances or for your own private clients.

One thing to note that is particularly satisfying about working with your own private clients is you get to help them. Help them try new things, help them become more confident, help them gain more self-respect and open their eyes to your passion, skills and knowledge.

But wait... how about becoming a celebrity

fashion stylist? Your job is to make your client look good from head to toe - you become their personal shopper, fashion consultant and style 'psychologist'!

* Not interested in dealing with red carpet diva dramas? Think about this list of options:

* Editorial styling

* Video or TV commercial styling

* Television

* Wardrobe stylist (under the direction of a costume designer - actors and actresses)

* Show styling (everything from public speaking to backstage, running orders and everything in between!)

* Live performance stylist

* Corporate styling (uniforms to personal appearance seminars)

* Personal shopping (my favourite!)

* Runway stylist

* Catalogue styling

* Retail fashion styling

* Prop and set styling

* Photo styling

* Merchandise stylist

Seriously, check out

www.australianstyleinstitute.com.au as one option

and get going!

The world needs your talents and I need help in

banning horizontal striped anything above size 14!

JOURNALISM

An old school friend of mine was always a smart little kitten through college. So when it came time to deciding on something to do at University to keep her parents smiling she chose journalism. Now... she is the Communications Director for the UN based in New York!

Just one of the many options available for someone who has a brain in their head, something to say and the ability to make a difference (I would like to think that this is at least 50% of the present population!)

Journalism is the art of learning how to extensively research, collate, then write and/or present your findings in hopefully an unbiased, objective and articulated manner. Gather your thoughts, put pen to paper (fingers on keyboard) and produce something that moves people to action, informs and educates or entertains - and if you're really good, all of the above in one sitting.

Journalists can enjoy a broad career with many opportunities within different areas of the media. You could become a reporter, a subeditor, editor, feature writer or photojournalist. You can appear in documentaries, on the news or in publications. You will need definite qualifications for this career choice as well as tenacity, a 'thick skin' and a serious thirst for knowledge and the truth.

MAKE UP ARTIST

By combining makeup and artistry you have one deadly combination for enhancement and reinvention. Makeup artists skillfully transform a human canvas into a desired character or appearance in no time.

Makeup artists normally possess a broad range of common skills and able to clearly enhance the client's natural features for a flawless finish. The training is ongoing for new products, styles and techniques.

Makeup artists need to have their own tools, be punctual, flexible, organised and great with people. Respected makeup artists are also regular guest beauty editors in magazines, add commentary, work with cosmetic companies and even create their own line of cosmetics - talk about leveraging a skill where there will always be a demand!

Makeup artistry is a diploma initiated career followed by a lot of on-the-job training, product training and development.

Specialised areas that employ makeup artists include:

* High fashion

* Theatrical

* Editorial

* Special effects

* Television

* Airbrushing

* Weddings

* Counter sales (retail)

* Prosthetics

* Mortician (creepy ... but it's a job!)

PHOTOGRAPHER

Let's start with the most obvious...

Photographers take pictures. Aren't you glad you bought this book?

But hold on a minute – there's more to being a photographer than taking pictures. There is the serious skill of understanding lighting. There's the editing, the styling, dealing with people, places, weather and other variables just to get "the shot."

Then there's the serious competition with every person with a mobile phone - so they compete with everyone! You have to be your own marketing machine. Photography is definitely an art form and as such, is worthy of publications, art galleries, the news and media.

Photographers are patient and see people, places and things differently to the rest of us. They can capture a moment or a feeling that can say a thousand words.

They have the honour of capturing history, beauty, pain and exhilaration in an instant.

Photographers quite often need to travel, work outdoors, in a studio and under stressful conditions. So before you get swept away with your new phone here are a few qualities and skills you will need.

* A love of photography - love what you do and you'll never work a day in your life!

* Knowledge - subjective and creative.

* Foresight - what will give you the best shot?

* Business savvy - very competitive.

* Learn about photography - steps, styles, techniques and theories.

* Appreciate the work of others - inspiration for new ideas.

Ask yourself, what lifestyle do you want: self-employed or working with employees? How are you going to build a portfolio, the bigger the better?

You'll need to sell yourself: don't wait for the work to come to you.

PUBLIC RELATIONS (PR) CONSULTANT

A PR consultant's job is all about communication and they invariably work with event managers to help get their message across.

The work is varied, high energy, responsive, involves planning, developing ideas and strategies, gathering information and ensuring that the message is received effectively by all mediums involved.

* Here are just some of the responsibilities a PR consultant may perform:

* Respond to inquiries from the public, media and other organisations

* Conduct internal communication workshops, course and media training

* Plan, develop and massage brand identity

* Monitor public opinion regarding an organisation or particular issues

* Write speeches, prepare visual aids and make public presentations

* Develop and implement communication strategies for a client or an organisation and advise management of these strategies

* Present arguments on behalf of a client to government, special interest groups and other organisations

* Oversee production of visual (film or video), audio and electronic material, including managing websites

* Organise special events such as open days, visits, functions and exhibitions

As you can see, a PR consultant is very busy and had to be able to effectively communicate both orally and in writing to a wide range of people. You need to be interested in people, have great analytical skills, be organised, enjoy current affairs and be able to work under pressure. Also be prepared to work long hours including evenings and weekends, as well as be available to travel if required.

PRODUCTION CO-ORDINATOR

Want to work in film or TV - just ***not in front*** of the camera? Well this could be something for you. You will assist the production manager or supervisors in organising (there's that word again) the business, finance and employment issues in TV and film productions. So yes, you need to be organised and be able to manage projects. You'll never get bored as these projects will be varied and change regularly.

Your work may include location scouting and provide casting, crew and facilities information.

You could be involved in office management, coordinating schedules, monitoring PR activities, supporting fundraising activities and tracking the project(s).

One spin off from this vocation is a **Media Production Manager**. This role is primarily about sticking to the shooting schedule and staying within budget. You need to be diplomatic, highly organised and be willing to work long hours to be great at this job.

Then there's the **Production Manager**. This lucky duck is an excellent communicator and extremely diplomatic due to the fact that he/she interacts with actors, directors and production employees on a daily basis.

You are also responsible for the safety of the cast and crew and ensure all OH&S and its guidelines are adhered to and appropriate licenses are attained. Making sure the project stays within budget, requires knowledge about the lighting, sound, editing and general production equipment being used -starting as an assistant and then moving to a production coordinator seems the best way to get into this never ending industry of possibilities.

PROMOTIONS MANAGER

The definition of 'promote' is to publicise and sell. A promotions manager quite often teams up with the advertising manager to deliver a responsive campaign for a product, service, industry or occasion.

In all cases it is imperative that the promotions manager and their team have a really good understanding about the industry, product, service or person they are promoting.

It is an awesome gig, which combines the strategy sessions of the office with the dynamic of being amongst the industry players. A promotions manager supervises and coordinates the client's external marketing and promotional activities. This vocation also lends itself to the promotions manager actually being the 'face' of the company in terms of promotional and community events.

And to avoid any 'bad press' the promotions manager uses their knowledge of local and state legislation to ensure the event, the advertising and all the reporting and disclosure requirements are adhered to standard.

Travel again is expected in this career as there are many ways in which to promote, create strategic alliances and keep up-to-date with the competition - something that is a priority for any manager.

SALESPERSON

In a past life I was told on a number of occasions that I "could sell ice to the Eskimos" - an oldie but a goody! From prestige cars to wholefoods to real estate - I sold it and was quite good at it for two reasons: I appreciated the value in what I sold, and I loved dealing with people. This type of career is all about differentiating yourself, building rapport and trust, developing relationships with clients, organisations and peers.

There are daily challenges faced from closing the sale, being responsive to demand and problem-solving /thinking on your feet which has a tendency to bring either the best or the worst in people. There are invariably sales goals to be reached each month with the added bonus of commission being the incentive.

Commission or 'GP' as we used to call it, allows you to potentially make A LOT more money on top of your retainer or base wage. It is also very much about the needs and wants of your customers, with referrals being a huge part of a successful sales career as well as over delivering value and support. Some familiarity with the basic sales cycle is also an advantage.

This cycle normally works like this:

Market research > Identification of prospective customer > Preparation > Introduction > Questioning > Confirm understanding > Selling the product/service > Trial close > Overcoming any objections > Close the sale > Ask for referrals

Learning to be a great salesperson comes mainly from the school of hard knocks, trial and error and a willingness to learn and apply. This career is the ultimate leveraging tool and one that will not only teach you about life, but can also set you up for life!

SET DESIGNER or SET BUILDER

I had absolutely no idea what a set designer did or that there was a difference between a set designer and a set builder, until I made a few calls and researched further to find that these career are the ultimate combination of art history, design, make-believe and sacrifice. Set designers get to design scenery for films, television, theatre, dance and other productions. From opera to Broadway, set designers have an absolute blast!

Many set designers are highly educated with degrees in art, art history, theatre production or specific set design qualifications. They normally start as a scenery assistant (through an internship or apprenticeship) and get experience with painting and carpentry until they are highly skilled in the required aesthetics of set design and function.

This craft requires a great deal of cooperation from the whole creative team.

Everyone to do with the lighting, costumes, special effects, engineers and the design team come together to produce the 'look and feel' of the production. Most importantly a set designer has to be able to visualise the finished product(s).

They have to be excellent communicators, be able to work independently and as part of a team. Something else to consider as a career is a Set Decorator. You are responsible for creating the detailed look at the set from the furniture and fittings to the items in the fridge or the litter on the street.

Both of these positions require the ability to visualise the director's vision, be extremely organised, be able to the budget, be highly resourceful and prepared to work long hours. Most successful set designers and decorators agree that their vocations are "not a job that one walks into, but a career that one builds up to". Hands-on experience and learning from an assistant position are invaluable when building a network of industry contacts and consequently building your career.

SPONSORSHIP MANAGER

To put it simply your role is to produce a win-win situation for all involved. The sponsorship manager is employed by either party, normally being a corporation and a media asset or a non-for profit/charity. Sponsorship deals are big business and involve a lot of preparation adding value and benefits to a proposal package for collaboration.

The sponsorship manager is in charge of the process and the initial development of the relationship. This position often begins at a marketing level position where you are assigned accounts with very little exposure. You work on these and build your skills until you are competent enough to deal with the 'big boys'. Endorsements and sponsorships can add up to billions of dollars worth of sales each year and each relationship is looked at with a long-term vision.

Essential benchmarks and milestones are met as per the objectives of the partnership. It is also the sponsorship manager's role to constantly look for new opportunities to further promote the partnership beyond what was originally envisaged. The team includes the marketing department, talent agents, Accounts department and management, so excellent communication skills are on top of the list as well as being able to determine the viability of a partnership. Remember, it's all about win-win!

TALENT AGENT

In my opinion there's nothing like discovering new talent and guiding them to steady work and success! Finding work in the creative fields can be extraordinarily difficult. Without an agent, in most circumstances, your chances of being paid to do something you love - artistically speaking comes down to talent, timing and a bit of luck.

Talent agents discover artists with talent, help them find paying work and negotiate their contracts. The agent and/or agency can represent models, sports stars, sculptors, singers, actors, painters, musicians, authors and even directors. A recruitment agent is the more mainstream version.

Being a talent agent requires a certain personality. You need to work long hours, be committed to your client's success and have many responsibilities. You create a large group of industry contacts whom you network with regularly. You hold auditions and get to know what your clients are looking for, then find the talent to suit.

Talent agents can work from anywhere -

BUT you and your talent need to be accessible to the main metropolitan areas as this is where the bulk of the work is. Having some experience in marketing, Human Resources or Public Relations is helpful in this industry but not essential. An internship at a respected talent agency will give you the opportunity get on-the-job experience as well as learn from successful professionals in the field.

Talent agents also have to be licensed with the license depending on the type of talent you are representing. So for example, you may need to be part of a *Screen Actors Guild* to represent actors.

One final note is to remember that as a talent agent you will not usually get paid until your talent has been paid. Most talent agents get paid 10 to 20% of what their clients make depending on the type of job and what has been confirmed in the contract.

TRAINER

This is one of my favourite things to do! I'm a qualified workplace trainer and assessor. I earned my Certificate IV Workplace Trainer and Assessor and I have been delivering and assessing courses in hospitality, enterprise education and grooming and deportment for over twenty years.

You need to be really organised, proficient in recognising and delivering to specific learning styles that are more than likely all in one room and possess the need to encourage and support 24/7, while at the same time being acutely aware of the present and future realities facing your participants.

A corporate trainer is a specialised skill development position in a corporation where the goal is to help improve the performance of employees. These performance areas can range from 'soft skills' or 'people skills' to 'hand skills' relating to specific technical tasks.

Non - profits and government organisations have use for a corporate trainer's services. Trainers help develop, pitch, organise and present workshops, PowerPoint presentations, challenges, goals and solutions for the corporation and their employees.

Employees can become corporate trainers through their expertise in a particular area they have an interest in, instruct and deliver and have a proven ability to achieve results for the employees, their clients as individuals and for the broader vision of the organisation as a whole.

CAREER TALK

How To Break Into Advertising

As told by Anne-Marie Clarke, National Advertising Manager of *Marie Claire Australia* (March 2014):

I did a double degree (Bachelor of Journalism and Bachelor of Business) at Queensland University of Technology, graduating in 2003 [to get into the business]. At the end of my university course, I was working for free at pretty much any company that would give me work experience! This really helped broaden my knowledge of the media industry and where I wanted to work. I quickly learnt that being journalist was not for me so I moved into PR and did some part-time work at a consultancy while I was finishing my degree. Towards the end of 2003,

I saw an ad in the paper for a Media Sales Cadetship at UNSW, and as I had always wanted to move to Sydney I applied and got in. I had researched Media Sales jobs and opportunities and the Cadetship also placed us within media organisations. Media Sales clicked for me straight away – it combined my love for the media, utilised my writing skills and also my business degree. I was fascinated with the business side of media, and landed my dream role after completing the course at the start of 2014– an Account Executive on Marie Claire magazine! It's so funny that I am now back here leading the Marie Claire sales team as this was truly the position I aspired to 10 years ago.

I think it's a lot harder to get your foot in the door now and post-GFC, fewer companies are putting on junior roles BUT there are now more opportunities across other media platforms (online, social media, etc.) and I am feeling that the industry in general is feeling a lot more buoyant now than it did a few years ago. My top tips are to network when you can and always be open to invitations to meet other people in your industry; to intern wherever you can so you get a sense of what sort of job you ideally want, and to also not say no to any opportunities that might not be your dream job straight away. After three months in my job at Marie Claire an opportunity came up on another magazine Better Homes and Gardens that the company wanted me to go for, and although that wasn't a brand that was on my radar at the time (I was 23!), the scope of it was enormous. I was selling across TV, magazine and online with some of the biggest companies in Australia and it gave me exposure to all the big media agencies at a young age. So you sometimes have to look beyond the brand to see what this is adding to your overall skill set!"

I love the fast-paced nature of this industry and that no day is ever the same! Working specifically for Marie Claire, we are exposed to amazing international brands, see all of the latest fashion and beauty products before they hit the stores and most importantly are working for a brand that empowers women! The ad industry is a super fun place to work in, there is definitely a lot of innovation going on right now too and it's an exciting place to be.

It can be a highly stressful environment, especially in sales where budgets need to be met and you do have to deal with all types of personalities. My best advice is to let it consume you too much and make sure you have a fulfilling life outside work!

Which brings us to the other key person - the Creative Director (CD). This lucky person is involved in and oversees the agency's creative process and product for clients within the team of copywriters, art directors and designers. The CD works with the AE to bring the client's marketing plan and ideas to life. The CD assigns projects to the team and keeps track of the completion time – because at the end of the day the 'buck' stops with them!

The CD has to be a multi-tasking wizard and also needs the following to be a success and earn the big bucks:

* Work with and manage a team of 'creative types.'

* Communicate efficiently and professionally with the team, the AE and management.

* Strong leadership skills.

* Be able to bring out the best in his team.

* Work long hours and stick to deadlines.

* Be prepared to take the blame if the project fails.

* Be highly proficient in the number of programs such as Photoshop, Illustrator, InDesign, Flash, PowerPoint and QuirkXpress.

* Willing to travel if required.

Most CDs have a Bachelor degree, they then start with an agency, building up their experience in copywriting and various design roles until they have the experience and confidence to be chosen for a position they apply for or are recommended for within an agency. Starting your own business is also an option.

Remix Your Qualifications As A Top DJ

As told by DJ Dakota (djdakota.com) (February 2014):

My father has always been a musician in a band, and my mother played piano, so music has always been around me. I took piano lessons she I was young for a little while and was a radio junkie, recording music off of the local stations. So, when I went to college, I began volunteering at the College Radio Station and my passion grew for the music from there. I began collecting 12" vinyl of my favourite dance music when I went backpacking in Europe and taught myself how to spin on tables that didn't have pitch control, because at the time, I couldn't afford Technic 1200's.

Because a Radio DJ had to be FCC-certified (Federal Communication Commission), this Certification was highly sought after and I began DJing in some of the top College Radio Stations in

Florida.

This eventually led to the Club scene and I DJed in Miami's clubs as a guest DJ. Every time I DJed, I handed out demos to the crowds and my reputation grew from there. I also impressed many key people in the crowd who got me prominent gigs in Miami for Nightlife magazine interviews, Premier parties, and TV Shows.

Always be positive and meet everyone with a smile. If something is not of your liking, don't do it, but graciously decline, so you don't burn any bridges. Continue to do what style or event you prefer to do, and do it well. Practice and practice. It's one thing to be good, but it's another to earn the respect of your industry. Also, be "in-tune" with your audience. Try to feel their energy and you will know if they are "with" you or not with your song choice and progression of the music. I do this by not clouding my sets by drinking too much, etc.

Music in the Universal Language and I've always felt so moved by it, that I've been drawn to it. I have always wanted to share this feeling with as many people as I could. The feedback has been incredible and this makes me so happy, because I know that it flows from the purist place in my heart, and the Universe…it's my Calling and you can tell when you hear my mixes. This makes me so happy when others feel what I feel.

Sadly, many people feel that you HAVE to use drugs to feel this feeling. That makes me sad, because it almost as though they didn't give their heart and their own positive energy its natural chance to feel this without drugs. I knew someone who had been addicted to drugs in the club scene and when he became clean, he couldn't listen to the music anymore because it tempted him too much to do drugs. This association is sad to me. I understand it, but it's a shame the music had to be silenced.

Also, there are so many egos in the industry and I feel that there is a lot of music to share and the more DJs to share it, the better. I also don't believe a DJ should "hide" a song by not telling anyone who it is, etc., and keep it just for himself/herself. The producer should get the proper recognition for doing a beautiful job in making a great song.

Become A Fashion Designer

As told by New Zealand fashion designer, author and philanthropist Annah Stretton (annahstretton.co.nz) (April 2014):

I entered in the business of fashion by a lot of happy accidents and I quickly learnt the importance of simply taking opportunities as they arose. I have never called or seen myself as a fashion designer, but rather I am in the business of fashion, as a result I employ fashion designers and very good ones that build on my creative ideas and allow me to focus on my business.

I have schooling history with an art focus, a painting drawing and sculpture, I then went on through a dare from my late father and brother to study accountancy, resulting in a full ACA degree. So I now, enviably have both sides of the brain functioning left and right (which is rare especially for creative people). From an accountancy role with a clothing company I merged into their creative side of the operations and three years later I decided to go out on my own, setting up on a farm just outside of Morrinsville to create what now is known today as the Annah Stretton brand.

The smart thing to do is to get lots and lots of knowledge before you go out on your own... learn at the expense of others make mistakes at the expense of others, I cannot stress enough the importance of learning from others …. offer yourself for free over all sort of platforms get involved in fashion shows, expos and most importantly develop a commercial edge to what you do, as at the end of the day you have to sell clothes to survive. Learn about the business of fashion don't leave others to do this for you. Always love what you do. If you don't love it, change it or get out.

Build your networks and find a mentor from the outset - find many mentors, talk to people. Even now I am still talking - you will never know it all.

Change – embrace it, we are always changing, from the styling content to the platforms of operation. Nothing is constant; nothing is ever the same, a new season and the flavour of the collection changes. The digital world is constantly opening up platforms of operation that are exciting.

The global world and all that it offers is even more enticing. After 21years I love what I do, the people ,the products and the environments, but I am always driving the outcomes and looking for the opportunities, I never become exhausted by all that is going on around me, quite the opposite it invigorates me. But change is key as to not change will cause demise. Embrace all that is so exciting about this industry and the associated digital world.

The disconnection and the lack of support for the fledgling designer, I have often referred to the fashion industry as an industry that eats it young. I am constantly amazed at the lack of support for the next generation, existing designers concerned about design protection and intellectual property, secret squirrel their operations, when some of the more established designers should simply trust the markets they have and assist others wanting to enter the industry with their dreams and vision.

Photography Beyond A Hobby

As told by Lauren Bath, photographer and self employed Integra entrepreneur (February 2014):

I got into photography through using the social media app, Integra. I began by taking photos on my phone and progressed to using a slur. Although I took a few introductory photography lessons the majority of my learning was done by taking photos and using Google.

My best advice to people landing their first shoot/ shoots is to do the best job that you can. You often only get one chance to impress people and you can never walk away having done less than your best. My first photographic job paid $400 and cost me $3000 to pull off. (New lens, new flash and 2x photography lessons.)

What is great about my position in the photographic industry is that I work in travel. I get paid to travel and take photos in the most amazing locations! My favourite place? Alberta, Canada.

The cons of the photographic industry are paperwork! For every amazing day spent shooting in some exotic location there is a day's worth of e-mailing, editing and office work.

What's It Like As A Makeup Artist?

As told by Kylie Eustace – Makeup artist, business owner, product creator (kylies.com.au) (March 2014)

I have always had a passion for colour and

makeup. I got into the makeup industry by Study, research, practice, work experience, more study and more practice.

Have motivation, passion, study, do work experience, practice, do use professional quality products, insure yourself, work on a great portfolio, only share work that is top quality, practice, watch experts , never stop learning and keep practising.

It is fun, creative and I love what I do. Getting lost with no GPS signal on the way to a job is the only bad thing.

Is PR Exciting?

As told by Nicole Crowley, author and PR executive in London and Sydney, BDM for Mantra Hotel Group (February 2014)

While true success in media and communications is largely dependent on sass, 'savviness', intuition and fast thinking, unfortunately a degree is usually required to get your foot in the door. I completed my Bachelor of Communication and Media studies with a major in Journalism which held me in good stead. The industry is fickle and competitive, so unless you have friends in high places, a degree won't be enough. I completed a short internship with a lifestyle agency in Sydney which was ultimately two-fold – I was able to learn the basics (and I do mean the basics; buying ribbon for invitations, counting inventory, taking notes,) and I was also able to use the agency as a trophy-name on my CV to increase my employability.

Any graduate will be hard-pressed to land an entry-level PR job in their desired field, let alone their desired agency. My advice would be to look for a PR role in a *PR agency* so that you are exposed to a range of clients with different needs and different projects; should you choose to move into a different field, you will have a wider range of experience to draw from. Equally important is finding a culture that is right for you. It's common to settle for the first role you're offered because you're in an enthused rush to kickstart your career, but don't kid yourself – it's a steep learning curve and there will be bumps along the way, so remember to treat your interviews as two-way conversations and ask about the potential for a mentor and additional training.

PR is a tumultuous but rewarding industry. It's no secret that the pool of editorial staff is shrinking and the nature of print publication is changing; for a PR whose job sits in the middle of the public and the news, it means you're in a very exciting space. More than ever, PRs are being called upon the help shape the news and are challenged to find new ways to sell-in their story. The life of a PR is a life of multi-tasking, so the great thing is variety: you will dash from event planning, to fire-fighting with crisis comms, to media release writing, to counselling (expect a melt-down or 10 from clients!), to new business pitching and media pitching – it's a never-ending wonderland.

Though sometimes contested, the reality is that PRs (*especially* in the early days) are over-worked and underpaid. Of course everyone believes this is true at some point in their career, but PR is undoubtedly one of those careers. As a junior PR, you can expect less than $50k for a minimum of nine hours a day, plus events, networking nights, peaks in project work if you are in fashion or sports industries. As a service industry, it is also likely that you will complete a daily timesheet which bills your clients. This is where passion rises and pulls you through – you either love it or hate it, you move on, or you move up.

The Life Of A Set Designer

As told by Adam Gardnir, set and costume designer, business owner (adamgardnir.wordpress.com) (February 2014)

I was 15 when I went to see a piece of theatre (a play by Nick Armfield) and that was it! I came out of the theatre and said to my mother "I am going to be a set designer!" I couldn't explain why at the time, now I refer to it as a realisation or a calling – it's what I wanted to do. I am from Newcastle and as much as it a great place to grow up, it was not very friendly towards artists. I found some independent jobs, but ended up enrolling in the Victorian College of the Arts (VCA) in Melbourne to study 3 years full time (The course is now 4 years full time).

I worked independently (that's for free!) and did other casual jobs to pay the bills for the first 5 years, then it all started to come together and by 7 years I was being paid for every job I did. I am also a draftsman and do 3D modelling work on the computer as well as assistance work for other senior designers. This supplements my income and keeps me engaged within the industry and with my peers.

I have to say I am the luckiest designer in Australia as I have been working solidly with no gaps since I left college – I have worked very hard to attain this and I am committed.

I have four rules that I live by and that I always tell students when I am deliver a speech.

Rule 1: Never over commit – Over commitment leads to Underworked/Unemployed.

Rule 2: Do everything you possibly can in your timeline while keeping with Rule 1! When I was starting out I took every job I knew I could do with the time I had because I never knew who it would introduce me to or where it would lead.

Rule 3: Phone a friend! I have found that if you need something done, are running late, need some help sourcing there is always someone that can help you out.

Rule 4: When you go into a meeting or are asked to apply for a job, always assume everyone in the room knows more than you do.

The next bit of advice is something that I have found to be true for me and I would say 99% of the Set Designers in this country.

You can have 2 out of the 4 outcomes here. An esteemed position and a good job. A good income. A good marriage. Good health.

My advice if you want all of these things as a Set Designer is to cross pollinate your workload, for example, work as a Set Designer some of the time and teach set design some of the time.

I LOVE IT! I love what I do… It's crazy, nutty, generally people are really lovely, it's an international industry so I am always travelling and while working when I travel my skills and I stay relevant and it's creative. I love being involved with people who do art and see art.

Quite a few of my fellow graduates also used their Arts degree as a stepping stone into other successful careers such as Advertising, Real Estate, Fashion Design and Communications and a stage manager friend of mine is now a head hunted PA working for the MD in a multinational firm.

You need to really want to do this and be involved in this industry – your level of commitment makes all the difference. There are long hours, late nights and you work when the work is on. I organise my holidays within 2 weeks of actually going and relationships tend to suffer, hence my 2 out 4 realisation.

More On Set Building

As told by Tim Blaikie, set builder, business owner (showworks.com.au) (February 2014)

I was a lapsed actor who had trained in carpentry, I decided to make a change in my career path and using the "list of 10"™ settled on set building. I started in a lowly position and worked my way up through the ranks.

Turn up early, work hard and be nice! Of 2 equally skilled staff members, the boss is always going to lay off the less pleasant one first. The good: the variety, creativity, freedom. The bad: this occupation is highly competitive and seasonal.

CLOSING NOTES

Where To Get Help For Eating Disorders

Australia

TheButterflyFoundation.org.au

ReachOut.com

PaulaKotowicz.com

USA

NationalEatingDisorders.org

UK

http://www.b-eat.co.uk

Similar to the Butterfly Foundation, BEAT is a UK charity organisation that provides services and support to those experiencing eating disorders, or issues with food, weight and shape.

South Africa

http://www.recoveryspace.org/home

The information on their website above appears appropriate and they seem to be preparing to run support group services. They may be able to tell you about other services available in RSA.

India

http://www.mindmantra.in

http://www.novasans.com/eating-disorder-treatment/india/

http://www.docgautham.com/disorders/anorexia

http://www.goravgupta.com/eating-disorder-treatment-delhi-india.php

http://indianpediatrics.net/may2007/may-357-359.htm

http://www.faythclinic.com/contact-us-locate-us/

Asia

http://www.heda-hk.org

Based in Hong Kong, there are also some internationally known researchers in the eating disorders space there.

Thank You!

People

All of the incredibly helpful and generous people I interviewed for this book and especially the PA's who listened to my story and passed on my e-mail (Thank you Jenny, Rachel, Wishna and Glenda)

Dr. Paul Cook – Alexander Technique, therapist (private) and practitioner at Gwinganna Retreat, QLD, Australia

Mr. Steve Harrison – Steve Harrison's publicity and publishing tips (e-newsletter)

Ms. Nicole Russin-McFarland, who is an amazingly talented young lady and brilliant journalist who published my first three articles ever!

My family and friends who supplied endless support and the occasional challenge.

Mrs. Paula Kotowicz for her never ending

energy, professionalism and limited time she made available for me.

Miss. Steph Bowe for reading my first manuscript on a train and offering me the feedback that made me step out of my comfort zone, believe in my message and create the book you have read.

Lucky Pineapple Books for publishing my work.

www.ingramcontent.com/pod-product-compliance
Lightning Source LLC
LaVergne TN
LVHW051046080426

835508LV00019B/1735